# PUSSY RIOT

**Eliot Borenstein** is Professor of Russian & Slavic Studies, Collegiate Professor in the Faculty of Arts and Sciences, and Senior Academic Convenor for the Global Network at New York University, USA. His first book, *Men without Women: Masculinity and Revolution in Russian Fiction, 1917–1919*, won the AATSEEL award for best work in literary scholarship in 2000. In 2007, he published *Overkill: Sex and Violence in Contemporary Russian Popular Culture*, which received the AWSS award for best book in Slavic Gender Studies in 2008. His latest book, *Plots against Russia: Conspiracy and Fantasy after Socialism*, came out in 2019. Borenstein was also the recipient of a Guggenheim Fellowship in 2009.

Published in a succinct, accessible format, *Russian Shorts* provides concise examinations of key concepts, personalities, and moments in Russian historical and cultural studies, encompassing its vast diversity from the origins of the Kievan state to Putin's Russia. Each thought-provoking and easily-absorbable volume is designed to provoke debate and conversation on a wide range of intriguing topics. The series introduces readers to a side of Russian history and culture they don't know, extending the boundaries of our understanding in the process.

**Published Titles**
*Pussy Riot: Speaking Punk to Power*, Eliot Borenstein
*Memory Politics and the Russian Civil War: Reds Versus Whites*, Marlene Laruelle and Margarita Karnysheva

**Upcoming Titles**
*Art, History and the Making of Russian National Identity: Vasily Surkiov, Viktor Vasnetsov, and the Remaking of the Past,* Stephen M. Norris
*Russia and the Jewish Question: A Modern History*, Robert Weinberg
*Russian Utopia: A Century of Revolutionary Possibilities*, Mark Steinberg
*The Soviet Gulag: History and Memory*, Jeffrey S. Hardy
*The Afterlife of the 'Soviet Man': Rethinking Homo Sovieticus*, Gulnaz Sharafutdinova
*The Origins of Racism in Russia*, Eugene M. Avrutin
*The Multiethnic Soviet Union and its Demise*, Brigid O'Keeffe
*Russian Food since 1800: Empire at Table*, Catriona Kelly
*Meanwhile, In Russia: Russian Memes and Viral Video Culture*, Eliot Borenstein

# PUSSY RIOT

## SPEAKING PUNK TO POWER

*Eliot Borenstein*

BLOOMSBURY ACADEMIC
LONDON • NEW YORK • OXFORD • NEW DELHI • SYDNEY

BLOOMSBURY ACADEMIC
Bloomsbury Publishing Plc
50 Bedford Square, London, WC1B 3DP, UK
1385 Broadway, New York, NY 10018, USA
29 Earlsfort Terrace, Dublin 2, Ireland

BLOOMSBURY, BLOOMSBURY ACADEMIC and the Diana logo are trademarks of
Bloomsbury Publishing Plc

First published in Great Britain 2021
Reprinted 2021 (twice), 2022

Cover design by: Tjaša Krivec
Cover image: Pussy Riot performs during a show as part of the Festival Ceremonia 2019
at Foro Pegaso on April 6, 2019 in Toluca, Mexico.
(© Medios y Media/Getty Images)

A catalogue record for this book is available from the British Library.

Library of Congress Cataloging-in-Publication Data
Names: Borenstein, Eliot, 1966– author.
Title: Pussy Riot : speaking punk to power / Eliot Borenstein.
Description: New York : Bloomsbury Academic, 2020. | Series: Russian shorts |
Includes bibliographical references and index.
Identifiers: LCCN 2020029968 (print) | LCCN 2020029969 (ebook) |
ISBN 9781350113541 (hardback) | ISBN 9781350113534 (paperback) |
ISBN 9781350113558 (ebook) | ISBN 9781350113565 (epub)
Subjects: LCSH: Pussy Riot (Musical group) | Protest movements–Russia (Federation–
Moscow–History–21st century.
Classification: LCC ML421.P88 B67 2020  (print) | LCC ML421.P88  (ebook) |
DDC 782.42166092/2 [B]–dc23
LC record available at https://lccn.loc.gov/2020029968
LC ebook record available at https://lccn.loc.gov/2020029969

| ISBN: | PB: | 978-1-3501-1353-4 |
| | HB: | 978-1-3501-1354-1 |
| | ePDF: | 978-1-3501-1355-8 |
| | eBook: | 978-1-3501-1356-5 |

Typeset by RefineCatch Limited, Bungay, Suffolk
Printed and bound in Great Britain

To find out more about our authors and books visit www.bloomsbury.com
and sign up for our newsletters.

*For Helena Goscilo,*
*Queen of all the riots*

*And in memory of Shana Nova Borenstein (1982–2020)*
*A riot girl from the day she was born*

# CONTENTS

# PREFACE

## A few words about words

In writing this book, I have attempted to make it comprehensible for the non-specialist. This means removing as many obstacles to understanding as possible, starting with questions of language. This book presumes no knowledge of Russian. Any Russian words are used sparingly, and Russian names are spelled in their most familiar and user-friendly English-language versions. Sources are cited in a variety of languages, but recommendations for further reading nearly always steer the reader towards English-language materials. All translations from the Russian are my own, unless otherwise noted.

When it comes to the three named members of Pussy Riot (Mariia Alyokhina, Ekaterina Samutsevich, and Nadezhda Tolokonnikova), I was obliged to make an uncomfortable choice. All three of these names are challenging to readers who do not know Russian, and in their public personas the women choose to refer to themselves by the informal short forms of their first names: Masha, Katya, and Nadya, respectively. And it is Masha, Katya, and Nadya who are discussed by their supporters on social media. Journalists, of course, use their surnames, while the only forum in which their full names and patronymics are the preferred form of address is the criminal justice system. When I refer to "Tokolonnikova," I feel like a judge or a prison guard.

So I have elected to call them what they call themselves, for simplicity's sake. But I cannot ignore the gendered implications of this choice (especially when writing about a feminist movement): using women's first names can look patronizing, particularly on the part of a male writer. In the end, I acknowledge the problem, but stand by my choice. In addition, I have decided to do the same for Nadya's ex-husband and activist comrade, Pyotr Verzilov. Though activists and friends refer to him as "Petya" (or even "Petya the Piggy," his "Voina" nickname), in the media he is almost always Verzilov. But his role in this book is limited to his position in Pussy Riot's orbit, so Petya he shall be.

Even more problematic is the word most often used to describe the young women in the Pussy Riot collective: girls. The Russian language, unlike English, has a particular word (*devushka*) used to describe a young woman from her late teens into her twenties. "Devushka" is decidedly not a "little girl," and calling her a woman in Russian is tantamount to adding a decade to her age. When speaking English, Nadya and Masha call themselves girls. As a member of an older feminist generation that was adamant about *not* calling adult women girls, I simply cannot follow suit. I was a student at Oberlin College in the 1980s, where using the word "girl" in this context was only slightly less objectionable than deploying a racial slur. I know that times have changed, and my much younger fellow Oberlin alumna Lena Dunham launched a career with a show about young women entitled "Girls," but I am either too old or not old enough to follow suit. Unless I am quoting, the women of Pussy Riot will be just that: women.

One more point about language, which I hope by now is obvious: readers who are squeamish about foul language might want to cover their eyes while turning the pages. Pussy Riot has had enough encounters with the censors; there is no need for Western academic publishing to join in on the suppression of their speech, or to be at all prim in discussing it.

Finally, a word about the approach taken in this book. While I try to provide as much information as I can in a book designed to be brief, I make no claims to objectivity. I provided simultaneous interpretation for an event featuring Petya and Pussy Riot's first team of lawyers (and my image was later used in Arkady Mamontov's third Pussy Riot documentary). I also spent some time with Nadya and Petya when they visited New York University. This book is my informed interpretation of the Pussy Riot phenomenon, and inevitably makes my own political convictions clear. *Pussy Riot: Speaking Punk to Power* is based on the premises that art is political, that dissent is patriotic, that church and state should be separate, and that authoritarian rule is worth opposing.

# ACKNOWLEDGMENTS

When the three Pussy Riot defendants were arrested in 2012, I knew I would eventually write something about them. But I never thought that I would still be doing so in 2019.

During that time, I have had the benefit of conversations and presentations on Pussy Riot with more people than I can possibly recall, but I will do my best. First of all, I would like to thank Yanni Kotsonis, the Founding Director of the Jordan Center for the Advanced Study of Russia. Yanni's work on the Jordan Center's first Pussy Riot event, as well as his input on establishing All the Russias, the Center's blog, made all of this work possible.

Among the people whose thoughts and input have been helpful along the way are: Barbara Browning, Julie Cassiday, Patrick Deer, Tatyana Efremova, Anna Fishzon, Ksenia Gorbenko, Bruce Grant, Maksim Hanukai, Katie Holt, Anastasia Kayiatos, Michael Kunichika, Christopher Labrot, Daniil Leiderman, Mark Lipovetsky, Tatyana Mikhailova, Anne Lounsbery, Leyla Rouhi, Suhdev Sandhu, Olga Shevchenko, Mark Steinberg, Jennifer Suchland, and Katrina vanden Heuvel. Special thanks to Elena Gapova for reading a draft of this book.

That initial Jordan Center event was co-sponsored by the Global Journalism Program at NYU (thanks to Brooke Kroeger), with logistical support from Patti Mouzatikis. I'm also grateful to Julie Cassiday for arranging another event at Williams College and Carol Ueland for inviting me to speak at Drew University. Joy Connolly, then Dean of Humanities at NYU, provided much-needed funding for my research.

Portions of *Pussy Riot: Speaking Punk to Power* appeared on the Jordan Center blog and the *Calvert Journal* website, and also in *Transgressive Women in Modern Russian and East European Cultures: From the Bad to the Blasphemous*, co-edited by Yana Hashamova, Beth Homlgren, and Mark Lipovetsky (Routledge, 2016).

At Bloomsbury, Eugene Avrutin, Rhodri Mogford, Stephen Norris, and Laura Reeves were incredibly supportive and helpful throughout

## Acknowledgments

every step of the process. I am also grateful to Mark Fisher for his skillful copyediting. Special thanks to the Russian, East European, and Eurasian Center (University of Illinois at Urbana-Champaign) for the summer grant that helped me complete this manuscript in a timely fashion.

As always, special thanks go to Frances Bernstein.

This book is dedicated to Helena Goscilo, a pioneer in virtually every area of Slavic Studies that matters to me: gender studies, media studies, and mass culture, just to name a few. Best of all, she has shown the world that if you can't enjoy yourself while doing your scholarship, you must be doing something wrong.

# INTRODUCTION: FOOLISH INCONSISTENCY

"You have to kill them with a cross before they get into the church. That's the point," explained the organizer of a Russian Orthodox youth festival in the summer of 2013.[1] He was describing a video game about Pussy Riot, the all-female punk activist collective that, after a year of minor internet fame for their public, guerrilla theater antics, shocked a nation by performing their anti-Putinist "Punk Prayer" in Moscow's Cathedral of Christ the Savior. By the time three of the participants were arrested and put on trial, Pussy Riot had become a household name. And, as the video game shows, not everyone was happy about it.

To be fair, pleasing the public was not on Pussy Riot's agenda. On the contrary, all of their public performances were designed to shock their audience out of their complacency. From that point of view, the Punk Prayer succeeded beyond their wildest expectations. It also landed three of their participants in jail.

## What happened

On February 21, 2012, five women entered the Cathedral of Christ the Savior, donned brightly hued balaclavas, and ran to the front of the church to begin their unsanctioned performance. Accompanied by the sound of a few recognizable punk chords on electric guitar and bass, the women alternated vigorous dancing with the posture of prayer (kneeling and crossing themselves), before being chased out by security guards. They made their way home, combined the short footage obtained at the cathedral with a more fleshed out (and less harried) performance recorded at another church, and released a video on the internet. On February 26, the state opened a criminal case, which led to the arrest of two women, Mariia (Masha) Alyokhina and Nadezhda (Nadya) Tolokonnikova six days later, and Yekaterina (Katya) Samutsevich on March 16.

Their trial for "premeditated hooliganism performed by an organized group of people motivated by religious hatred or hostility" began in Moscow's Khamovniki District Court on July 30. The prosecution brought in a parade of witnesses and experts testifying to the emotional damage done by Pussy Riot and their allegedly blasphemous pronouncements. None of the defense's expert witnesses were allowed to testify. On August 17, the three women were sentenced to two years in a prison colony. The defendants appealed, and in October, Katya dismissed her lawyers, hired a new one, and saw her sentence suspended on a technicality (she had trouble opening her guitar case and never made it to the solea, the disputed area of the church reserved only for (male) priests).[2] Nadya and Masha were sent to different, far-off prison colonies, and eventually granted early release on December 23, 2013, presumably to remove the issue from the international agenda in anticipation of the upcoming Winter Olympics that Russia would host in Sochi.

Since then, Masha and Nadya have founded two large-scale projects: Zona Prava, whose goal is to expose and challenge abuses in Russia's prison system, and Media Zona, an independent, internet-based news outlet. They have also, together and separately, produced and starred in a series of music videos. Masha wrote a memoir and performed in the world tour of the play she wrote about her experiences, while Nadya published *Read and Riot: A Pussy Riot Guide to Activism*. Katya has stayed clear of the public spotlight, and most of the other members of Pussy Riot have remained anonymous. Masha's former common-law husband, Pyotr (Petya) Verzilov, who had been part of Pussy Riot's support system, co-founded Media Zona, and continued to take part in Pussy Riot-related public actions. In September 2018, he nearly died after an alleged poisoning, and was flown to Germany for treatment.[3]

The mere facts of the Pussy Riot story tell us little. In particular, they do not explain how Pussy Riot became a worldwide sensation, nor what the Pussy Riot trial meant for Russians who supported

Russian President Vladimir Putin and for Russians who opposed him. How did a political/artistic prank by a group of masked young women lead to heartfelt statements of support by Madonna and Paul McCartney, invitations to meet Hillary Clinton, and a guest-starring gig on the Netflix drama *House of Cards*? This was a time when the Russian Federation had not been prominent in the news of the world. Just one month after Pussy Riot's Punk Prayer, when US Republican presidential candidate Mitt Romney asserted that Russia represented the biggest geopolitical threat facing his country, he was met with widespread derision (Obama retorted that "the 1980s [were] calling to ask for their foreign policy back").[4] But by the time their trial began, the Pussy Riot affair was tarnishing relations with the United States and much of Europe. Wherever Putin traveled, he was met with signs demanding Pussy Riot's release. Meanwhile, back at home, Putin's government had been dealing with a wave of protests that, while small when compared to the recent Arab Spring, were without precedent in twenty-first-century Russia.

## What happened before

Before we can unpack the significance of Pussy Riot and their Punk Prayer, we need to understand the system that their protest targeted. And that requires a small dose of history.

When Soviet General Secretary Mikhail Gorbachev initiated the program called "perestroika" in the mid-1980s, his attempt to modernize and liberalize the Soviet Union's one-party political system and centrally planned economy led to consequences he could never have foreseen (unless we believe the Russian conspiracy theory that Gorbachev was an agent paid by the US State Department to destroy the USSR, in which case the plan worked without a hitch). New artistic and political freedoms, combined with separatist movements and economic instability, eventually resulted in a botched 1991 coup attempt by Communist Party hardliners against Gorbachev and the subsequent dismantling of the Soviet Union by the year's end. The largest of the 15 countries to emerge from the Soviet rubble was the

Russian Federation, now led by former-communist-turned-liberal-firebrand Boris Yeltsin.[5]

Yeltsin's government initiated a massive privatization plan that facilitated the accumulation of wealth by a small number of well-connected, largely corrupt businessmen. Living standards plummeted, war broke out in the breakaway republic of Chechnya (leading to several spectacular acts of terror), and crime soared in a land previously noted for law and order. This was also a time of great artistic and political freedom, although few in the country took comfort in this fact. The increasingly drunk and addled Yeltsin stepped down at the beginning of the new millennium in favor of the fifth man to serve as his Prime Minister, Vladimir Vladimirovich Putin, a former KGB officer largely unknown to the public before the previous year.[6]

During his first two terms as president (2000–2008), Putin consolidated power in a system that had previously been moving in the direction of de-centralization. Regional governors were now appointed rather than elected; the previously powerful oligarchs (rich businessmen who were presumed to have undue influence on politics and government) were either chased out of the country, jailed, or coopted; another bloody war was fought in Chechnya (this time crushing the separatists but ceding nearly limitless power to a brutal thug loyal to Putin); nearly all independent media outlets were closed or brought under state control; and several prominent journalists were killed under mysterious circumstances. At the same time, Putin enjoyed unprecedented personal and political popularity: thanks to skyrocketing oil prices, the living standards and purchasing power of the general population rose for the first time in years. There was a general sense of increased order and stability, as if the people and state had tacitly agreed upon a grand bargain: the people (and especially educated elites) will stay out of politics, and the state will, for the most part, stay out of people's lives. An increasingly authoritarian government was paired with the mass culture of an open society.

Russia's constitution restricted presidents to two consecutive terms, and in 2008, Putin stepped down in favor of his Prime Minister, Dmitri Medvedev, who easily won election to the presidency. Putin was immediately appointed Prime Minister and widely presumed to be running the show, but Medvedev's infatuation with gadgets, the internet, and the trappings of liberal democracy left room for hope that he would lead the country in a less authoritarian direction. These hopes were dashed in 2011, when Medvedev proposed that the ruling United Russia party run Putin as their presidential candidate rather than Medvedev, as part of a deal the two men had cut long ago. This rather cynical move, followed by parliamentary elections tainted by gross instances of fraud (ballot box stuffing, buses full of repeat voters brought from one polling station to another), led to the largest Russian street protests since the new century began.

These protests were something new. For one thing, many of the people shown on television were young, well-dressed professionals—the very people who presumably could have been considered the beneficiaries of Putin's prosperity. For another, they displayed none of the solemnity of the public demonstrations of previous decades. The Soviet dissidents spoke the same political language as the regime they fought, calling on the USSR to honor its international commitments to human rights and appealing to the humanistic values their country claimed to espouse. The protesters of 2011–2012 seemed to understand the pointlessness of arguing with Russia's leaders on their own terms; their placards were often humorous, a rejection of the very seriousness the regime tried to project ("Don't rock the boat; our rat is sick"; "You don't represent us" (a play on words that also means "You can't even imagine us"). Against a regime that tried to hide its own ridiculousness under a veneer of pompous patriotism, the protesters weaponized absurdity.

On March 12, 2012, just three weeks after the Pussy Riot's Punk Prayer implored the Mother of God to cast him out, Putin won the presidential election. The protests, which continued into the next year, seem to have shaken the once and future president; during his acceptance speech, he struck the competitive, paranoid tone that would characterize his entire third term: "We have shown indeed, that no one can enslave us ... We have shown that our people are truly able to distinguish between the desire for progress and renewed political provocation that has only one objective—to destroy Russian sovereignty and usurp power."[7] The "March of Millions," a protest on

Moscow's Bolotnaya ("Swampy") Square, two months later, resulted in the arrest of 30 people on charges of violence against the police and 14 prison sentences. The increasingly harsh penalties for unsanctioned protest did their job; by the end of 2013, street protests were a much smaller and more sporadic affair.[8]

This was not for lack of a reason to protest; on the contrary, the Duma (the lower house of parliament) spent much of Putin's third term proposing and passing a series of repressive laws at such a brisk pace that the parliament was nicknamed the "mad printer": forcing non-governmental organizations that received foreign funding to register as "foreign agents"; banning "homosexual propaganda" in the presence of minors (while homosexual activity was not criminalized, saying positive things about homosexuality effectively was); increased controls and restrictions on the internet; and a moratorium on adoption of Russian children by American citizens. At the same time, construction and publicity efforts were going into overdrive in preparation for the 2014 Winter Olympics held in the Russian city of Sochi, an outpouring of federal money that looked unlikely to yield any long-term benefits to the region. The Winter Olympics took place in February, the same month that Ukrainian protesters finally ousted President Viktor Yanukovych, initiating a chain of events that would lead to separatist movements in Eastern Ukraine (with unofficial support from Moscow), and the Russian annexation of Crimea. Russia's relations with the United States and NATO quickly deteriorated, while a patriotic fervor swept the country.

Meanwhile, the Pussy Riot case was not going away. Inadvertently, the trial brought into focus the very issue that sparked the Punk Prayer in the first place: the unconstitutional erosion of the boundary between church and state. The defendants were charged with "hooliganism" (the equivalent of "creating a disturbance"), a catch-all category dating back to Soviet days. But the substance of the testimony against them centered on blasphemy and "satanic" disrespect for the Russian Orthodox Church. In 2013, while Nadya and Masha were still in prison, the Duma passed yet another piece of restrictive legislation, this time making it a crime to "hurt the feelings of religious believers."

## Why Pussy Riot matters

Pussy Riot was bold, clever, obscene, and—most jarring for Russians—feminist. In today's Russia, what could be more punk than radical feminism? The group's very name is a challenge to norms of sexual propriety and linguistic purity: an English rather than Russian phrase, "Pussy Riot" obliges Russian pundits, priests, and presidents to repeat a word that is still shocking to many English speakers, a term that Russians might not have even known before. The word is even more disruptive in the US and the UK: how do you report on a group whose official title might not get past the average spam filter?

Indeed, the name is something of a transnational scandal, a Russian phenomenon whose English designation redefined the limits of lexical acceptability on American network television news. If nothing else, the refusal by *NBC Nightly News* anchor Brian Williams to even pronounce the word "pussy" (after previously referring to Tolokonnikova and Alyokhina only as "two young women") was an entertaining performance in its own right.[9] "Pussy" existed in something of a twilight zone for network television, sayable and unsayable at the same time: the word was sometimes acceptable, but *only* as a term of abuse, and not an anatomical description.[10]

Meanwhile, in an interview with *Russia Today* (the state's propaganda network for English-language viewers throughout the world), Putin himself challenged his British interviewer to translate "Pussy Riot" into Russian (a challenge the interviewer declined), in an attempt to emphasize the group's vulgarity without being forced to articulate it himself ("I thought it was referring to a cat"). No stranger to the power of words, Putin remarked, "These people made everyone say their name too many times. It's obscene."[11] The Russian equivalent (*"pizda"*) has the harshness of the English "cunt," and, used as an obscenity, is laden with precisely the misogyny that Pussy Riot is attempting to combat. English-language attempts at reclaiming the term have been something of an uphill battle, but at least the term has been printable for decades (even if within limits).[12] The taboo on printing or broadcasting the Russian word is far stronger.

What gets lost when Pussy Riot crosses Russian borders and enters into the world mediascape is context. Pussy Riot has all the ingredients for a perfect media storm: viral video, feminist activism, delicate religious sensibilities, state persecution, and, of course, balaclavas. But the Western media and culture industry have done a middling job explaining exactly what Pussy Riot is. Is the Pussy Riot story about the stifling of avant-garde artistic expression? A crackdown on a new generation of dissidents? The unchecked power of the Russian Orthodox Church? The tragedy of three modern-day Joans of Arc who happen to curse like sailors?

Pussy Riot is resolutely uninterested in definitions and consistency.[13] In *Read & Riot: A Pussy Riot Guide to Activism* (2018), Nadya tells a story about Dmitri Prigov, the Moscow Conceptualist writer/artist who inspired many of the people associated with Pussy Riot, and was a personal hero of Nadya's. When Prigov was called a painter, he objected, "No, I'm a poet!" When he was called a poet, he responded that this must be a misunderstanding: after all, he is a sculptor. No matter what anyone called him, he insisted he was something else. While not exactly copying Prigov's shtick, Pussy Riot clearly operated according to a similar strategy.

Nearly every attempt at a pithy characterization of Pussy Riot fails, defeated by oversimplification. Either Pussy Riot is a "band," a group of "dissidents," "feminists", or "performance artists," but none of these terms is adequate on its own. One of the most famous thought experiments in modern physics concerns a cat in a box, suspended in an indeterminate state that renders it somehow simultaneously alive and dead. Perhaps Pussy Riot occupies a similar superposition, enjoying the benefits of quantum indeterminacy. Or perhaps any such experiment would be inappropriate: no one is putting this particular pussy in a box. Even behind bars, Pussy Riot projected an aura of radical freedom.

## What this book is, and what it is not

A short book on Pussy Riot cannot claim to cover everything, nor should it even try. Readers of *Pussy Riot: Speaking Punk to Power* will, of course, learn the basic story, from the group's origins through the trial and on to its aftermath. But this is not a comprehensive narrative of the events. For that, I recommend Masha Gessen's *Words Will Break Cement: The Passion of Pussy Riot*. Gessen's access to the group remains unrivaled, and the story she tells is both compelling and satisfying. Instead, this book focuses on the things that made Pussy Riot such an important phenomenon.

Pussy Riot has very often been framed—or unmasked—in the West in the familiar terms of punk. But rushing to identify them with various generations of punk performativity risks obscuring the specific power and wider implications of what they were doing in their "Punk Prayer" in the cathedral. Their art also needs to be understood in terms of their engagement with the discursive conventions of Russian and Soviet era dissident speech; the gender politics of Russian art activism; protest, Holy Foolishness, and the Orthodox Church; the challenge both to the political order and the politics of celebrity inherent in their use of masks and anonymity in the era of surveillance, censorship and viral internet video. By hesitating before the rush to declare Pussy Riot punk in familiar terms, we can pose some larger questions about the relationship between performance, activism and political repression.

After examining its roots in Actionism and the Russian protest scene, we will look at the complicated negotiations between the language of punk and the language of political dissidence, the tensions between live performance and viral video, the group's commitment to feminism in a decidedly anti-feminist context, and the problem of anonymity in a world obsessed with celebrity. By the end of this book, the reader will no doubt have learned a fair amount about Katya, Nadya and Masha, but their individual stories do not, on their own, add up to the phenomenon of Pussy Riot, nor should they overshadow the artistic and political actions performed by this anonymous collective. As we shall see, Pussy Riot is ill-served by fame, and far more comfortable in its natural habitat of infamy.

# CHAPTER 1
## PENIS RIOT: PUSSY RIOT'S PRE-FEMINIST ROOTS

### Declarations of war

To many observers (both foreign and domestic), Pussy Riot seemed to come out of nowhere. As we shall see in Chapter 9, while feminism has deep roots in modern Russia, it was far from popular in 2012. And even if one imagined growing unrest after over a decade of Putinism, the most obvious Russian precedent was the dissidents of the 1960s and 1970s: serious, often bearded intellectuals who laid out their claims against the regime in reasoned, persuasive language, with nary a balaclava in the bunch. If Putin-era Russia were a novel, the sudden appearance of masked feminist punk avengers would be a sign that the author has lost the thread of the plot.

Pussy Riot becomes more understandable (if not predictable) in light of a counter-history of Russian artistic dissent. As the Soviet writer Andrei Sinyavsky (Abram Tertz) said in a 2010 interview not long after he was exiled from his homeland, "My differences with the Soviet authorities were purely stylistic."[1] The last 25 years of Soviet power saw the rise of postmodernist artistic movements whose unconventional practitioners, though clearly disapproving of their country's political system, chose playful, oblique artistic expression over straightforward political critique. Chief among these were the Moscow Conceptualists, such as Dmitri Prigov (mentioned in the Introduction), the artist Ilya Kabakov, the poet Lev Rubinshtein, and the painters Komar and Melamid. Prigov and Rubinshtein's written work tended towards the whimsical and the irreverent, while Komar and Melamid took the classic paintings of socialist realism (official Soviet art) and distorted them by adding toy dinosaurs, renaissance motifs, and, in one case, E.T. the Extraterrestrial.[2]

The generation that followed them was also schooled in the philosophy of the Situationist International (1957–1972), a primarily French movement holding that advanced capitalism had replaced the individual, lived experience with commodity consumption and spectacle. The Situationists mounted public events according to the principle of "détournement" ("misappropriation", "diversion"), essentially turning the symbols of mass culture against themselves through pranks and parody.[3,4] The legacy of the Situationists can be felt throughout the world of left-wing political activism and art, from the activities of LGBTQI groups such as ACT-UP and Queer Nation to Emma Sulkowicz's "Mattress Performance: Carry that Weight" (carrying a mattress with them as a Columbia University undergraduate to protest what they saw as their university's indifference to sexual assault), to the Guerrilla Girls (an anonymous group of women who wore gorilla masks and demonstrated against sexism in the art world).

But the movement with which Pussy Riot most closely identifies is called Actionism. Founded in Austria in the 1960s, Viennese Actionism was one of the first waves of performance art, in this case rejecting art as an object in favor of art as an event. The Viennese Actionists were (in)famous for their violations of both law and decorum, often performing nude and occasionally publicly masturbating. They defied any sense of boundary between life and art, public and private, valuing transgression both as an attack on conventional, consumerist morality and for its own sake.[5]

In Russia, Actionism arose in the 1980s, allegedly independent of its Viennese predecessor, but with a great deal in common. The Moscow Actionists also emphasized transgression, and cultivated media exposure of their violations of social norms. In 1991, a group of Actionists, in response to a proposed law banning the use of foul language in public, lay their bodies down outside of Lenin's Mausoleum in order to spell "Хуй" ("Cock"), one of the most offensive words in the Russian language. Probably the most famous of the Moscow Actionists is Oleg Kulik, who gained notoriety by performing naked and pretending to be a dog (even going so far as to bite a viewer who disregarded the "Dangerous" warning sign to which he was chained).[6]

In 2007, inspired by Situationism, Actionism, and Moscow Conceptualism, Oleg Vorotnikov and Natalia Sokolova founded Voina ("War"), an anarchist, activist art collective whose members rejected participation in the mundane world of capital, wage labor, and consumerism (shoplifting was not just encouraged, but considered a "form of art"). Among the earliest members of the group were Petya, Nadya, and Katya. The year 2009 saw a schism divide the group (with Vorotnikov accusing Petya of being a police informant), leading to the formation of two separate Voina groups who refused to recognize each other's legitimacy: Vorotnikov's in Petersburg, and Petya's in Moscow.[7]

No matter the city, Voina created "actions" that were irreverent, politically challenging, and often hilariously funny. Not to mention obscene: Voina proudly deployed what the Russian media primly calls "non-normative vocabulary," crude sexual imagery, and the naked human body (with emphasis on nearly all its orifices). While many of their notable pranks had nothing to do with sex (such as their 2007 celebration of International Worker's Day involving throwing live cats at McDonald's cashiers), the more (porno)graphic actions not only attracted more activity, but also illuminate the path that led Nadya and Katya from Voina to Pussy Riot.

## All power to the phallus

As the actionist group that would eventually eclipse Voina, Pussy Riot's very name announces a shift in focus based on each group's understanding of gendered bodily realities. Pussy Riot owes a debt to French feminism's insistence on grounding feminist politics in the female body itself, whereas Voina's gendered priorities were largely unexamined. Here it is Pussy Riot, rather than Voina, that proves to be the best student of their beloved Situationists, since the name itself represents something of a *détournement* in the bodily discourse of power.

The history of Voina is the history of a struggle between two charismatic men in two different cities to define the agenda of this actionist movement (one of those men being Petya), with the sexualized imagery employed in their actions being primarily masculine-focused. To put it bluntly, before Pussy Riot, Russian Actionism was a celebration of the phallus. In May 2009, Voina occupied the Tagansky courtroom in Moscow, claiming to be a punk group called "A Cock Up the Asshole"; a few of the men performed a song called "Remember, All Cops are Bastards," while the rest of the group danced wildly. All three of the future Pussy Riot defendants took part in the dancing, little knowing that they would eventually headline a much more famous punk act of their own. But despite the presence of women, the whole event was structured around not just male sexuality, but male sexual violence. Thanks to the magic of Russian grammar, it's clear in the original that the group's name is about the *act* of inserting the aforementioned cock, rather than its simple location. The name is as much a threat as it is a description.

In 2010, the Petersburg wing of Voina painted an enormous phallus on a drawbridge opposite FSB headquarters, in an event called "Cock Captured by the FSB." As the bridge went up, so, too, did the phallus. But Voina's most notorious sexual performance took place in February 2008, the day before the presidential election (in which Prime Minister Dmitri Medvedev's victory was a foregone conclusion). An obvious reference to the future president's last name ("Medved" in Russian means "bear"), "Fuck for the Puppy Bear Heir" consisted of five heterosexual couples having sex in Moscow's Biological Museum. This is one of Voina's most notorious actions, and not only because of the very public sex. One of the couples was Petya and a very pregnant Nadya (she would give birth to their daughter Gera only a few weeks later). The Pussy Riot affair revived public attention to the event, which helped frame Nadya as a "slut" and a "bad mother."

Was "Fuck for the Puppy Bear Heir" pornography, as its detractors would call it? If we set aside the implicit anti-pornographic value judgment implicit in the accusation, then the answer is both yes and no. In porn, the actors and actresses at least pretend to be enjoying themselves, a feat managed by only one of the five couples (for the record, it was the one on the far left).[8] A better critique would be on the grounds of gender. "Puppy Bear Heir" was a study in patriarchal power dynamics; it seemed not to have occurred to anyone involved that there could be a sex act that did not involve penetration by a penis. There may have been a practical reason, given that anyone viewing the video is treated to the spectacle of the men grimly trying to get into (and maintain) the proper frame of mind—the men's steely determination was less like the demeanor of the stars of PornHub, and more reminiscent of the British prime minister at the end of the notorious bestiality-themed first episode of the dystopian TV show *Black Mirror*. Clearly, they needed all the help they could get. Still, even if we allow for the fact that Voina was exploiting a clear patriarchal metaphor of power (who gets fucked by whom), the video displays a marked lack of sexual imagination. Cunnilingus, it seems, is the love that dare not speak its name, and not only because the mouth is otherwise occupied.

If the biological museum event can safely be called pornographic, it is not as a value judgment, but as a performance that followed the most important imperative of filmed heterosexual porn—all power to the penis. Indeed, power is precisely the point. The use of the word "fuck" as an insult or even a political criticism implicitly assumes that the object of the verb is not just grammatically, but inherently passive, with penetration a metaphor for triumph and penetration (Valerie Sperling calls this the rhetoric of "topping," shared by the regime and opposition alike).[9] Perhaps inadvertently, the Petersburg wing of Voina's drawbridge stunt makes this fact even clearer: tracing a giant penis on public property is a classic "fuck you" gesture, but it is also one that inherently reinforces a gendered hierarchy.

This is what makes Pussy Riot's very name so radical. Unless it is reclaimed, the English word "pussy" is the antithesis of this macho "fuck you" gesture. As a term of abuse, it labels a person (usually a man) weak, cowardly, ineffective, flaccid. Patriarchal biological metaphors leave little room for female physical power: if so many actual weapons are phallic shaped (speak softly and carry a big stick), what kind of weapon is a pussy? Maybe we will live to see the day when soldiers fight each other with giant metal vaginas, but it is neither ideologically nor aerodynamically likely.

No one says "fuck you" with a vagina—the cock is the weapon of war (that is, of Voina). Pussy Riot is the scandal of female self-assertion, an attempt to say "fuck you" to authority while neither appropriating a phallic stance in a kind of transgender prosthesis, nor resorting to the readily available, maternal means of feminine resistance sanctioned by the culture at large (the mourning mother, à la the women in black).[10] By speaking the unspeakable of female anatomy, Pussy Riot uses the very name of the primary female sexual organ as its weapon against power. It may not be as easy to draw on the back of a bridge, but it is a far greater challenge to propriety. It takes a pussy to fight a dick.

Voina was characterized by a much more traditional gendered hierarchy. The leaders were men, and their concerns were phallic. The most dramatic exception would take place in Petersburg, one year after the Voina schism, Elena Kostyleva (half of the enthusiastic couple at the Biological Museum), shoplifted a frozen chicken by inserting it into her vagina in a videotaped event called "Why They Snatched the Chicken."[11] In the Moscow faction, however, both women and women's bodies were a secondary concern.

It is noteworthy, then, that one of the last actions performed by Voina before it would be eclipsed by Pussy Riot was entirely performed by women. And not just any women—the two most visible participants were Katya and Nadya. Entitled "Kiss a Pig" ("Лобзай мусора"), this was a series of public interactions with female militia officers over the course of January and February 2011, complied in honor of the upcoming March 1 law changing the "militia" into the "police" (by coincidence, this was also one week before International Women's Day, when Russian women are usually given flowers and chocolates by the men in their lives). The women of Voina approached female officers and, without warning, planted kisses on them (on the lips when possible, but anywhere else on the face would do).

In an interview with the LGBT magazine *Kvir (Queer)*, Nadya and Katya explained that the action was both a critique of the Russian police (Nadya: "We used physical contact to embody the well-known liberal slogan, 'The Militia is with the people!'") as well as homophobia.[12] The same-sex nature of the action must also have had a practical component: a man forcefully kissing a female officer would be immediately presumed to be engaged in sexual assault, while a woman kissing a man might not have been able to guarantee her own safety.

The same may well hold true for men attempting to kiss men, who could have a reasonable fear of a beating. According to Nadya, most of the men in Voina refused to take part, and those who agreed disappeared when it came time to do the preparatory training ("the next day they would tell us they broke their legs slipping on a banana peel along the way").

Yet actually watching the "Kiss a Pig" video is profoundly uncomfortable in a way that even watching "Fuck for the Puppy Bear Heir" is not. It would be too easy to ascribe such discomfort to changes in consciousness in the wake of the "#MeToo" movement; "#MeToo" was the widespread *confirmation* of the pervasiveness of sexual harassment and assault, not its discovery. It does not take a refined feminist consciousness to see that many of the female police officers kissed by Voina look terrified. Sperling, who interviewed activists from the Moscow Feminist Group (MGF), reports their condemnation of Voina's tactics.[13] One of them, Elizaveta Morozova, assets that Voina's symbolic struggle with the regime resorted to "very typical patriarchal tactics": "It's like, 'We're raping your women because you, the police, it's as if you're raping us as a country.' It's absolutely, openly, that kind of discourse."

This critique is consistent with Nadya's defense of the action in her *Kvir* interview: "When a person puts on a militia uniform, he stops being an ordinary citizen. You're a cop, you're a representative of the state, you're its executive organ, you're its leg and its member."[14] The unwillingness to see the women kissed as *women*, with the fear of sexual assault with which women live every day, is a serious blind spot. And an ironic one, especially for an interview with a queer publication. When talking about the policewomen, Nadya notes that they, surprisingly, turned out to be more "homophobic" than the policemen. But homophobia in this case is a red herring. Nadya and the women of Voina who took part in "Kiss the Pig" cannot see their actions as at least homologous to assault because they seem to be capitulating to a heteronormative framework: if there is no penis involved, there is no assault.

By the time they arranged "Kiss the Pig," Nadya had been reading widely in feminist theory and queer theory.[15] As a first step in feminist activism, "Kiss the Pig" was significantly flawed by its unacknowledged heteronormativity and its dismissal of the fundamental issue of consent. It was also the first, but not the last, action by Nadya and her comrades which would divide the Russian feminist community. Though they never repudiated "Kiss the Pig," the women of Pussy Riot clearly learned from it: Pussy Riot's subsequent performances did not involve deliberate physical contact with unsuspecting audience participants. A sympathetic reading of "Kiss the Pig" would be to acknowledge, as the Russian saying would have it, that this was the first pancake that never comes out quite right, and move on.

Barely a year after "Kiss the Pig," Nadya, Katya, Masha, and the other women of Pussy Riot had succeeded in completely flipping the gender script followed by Voina. "Remember, All Cops Are Bastards" had men playing the music on their guitars while the "girls" literally danced to their tune. "Teddy Bear Heir" displayed men confronting a very primal performance anxiety, with the women providing cooperative orifices or simply playing fluffer. Pussy Riot, on the other hand, needed no man's help to put them in the performing mood; indeed, if we follow the sexual metaphor further, the Punk Prayer, with its lip-syncing and overdubbing from a performance in a much less controversial church, was video evidence not of a crime (the state's imagination of the action's climax), but of the women faking one. And as for the men of Voina? While the women danced on stage, Petya was left to follow them around with his camera.

# CHAPTER 2
# INCITING A PUSSY RIOT

In September of 2011, Nadya and Katya spoke at an opposition conference, and chose to talk about feminist art. Most of their examples were from the West, which was frustrating: Russia, after all, did have a feminist history, most notably in the decades immediately before and after the 1917 October Revolution, but for the past seventy years, feminism had been virtually a dirty word. Women had entered the workforce, but without any discussions of how gender roles might (or should) change at home, resulting in a double burden: after coming home from work, women had to provide virtually all the domestic labor. Meanwhile, the late Soviet press in the 1960s and 1970s was paying more attention to the "man problem" than the "women problem," lamenting men's "infantilization" and their inadequacy at performing their "natural" leadership role.[1] When the Soviet Union was dismantled, the world of business was established as a man's game. Marrying a rich man and setting up house were presented as the stuff of the average woman's dreams.

But not those of Nadya and Katya. Instead, they found themselves in the position of wanting to end their lecture with a discussion of Russian feminist punk, which, at this point, was simply a product of their imagination. So, in the best traditions of the (nontraditional) avant-garde, they made one up. Calling it "Pisya Riot" ("pisya" is Russian baby talk for any genitalia, male or female), they closed the presentation with a brief introduction to the group, and then played a recording. To anyone who is familiar with the subsequent Pussy Riot *oeuvre*, it's obvious that the voices in the recording are those of Nadya and Katya themselves, but with the benefit of that very same hindsight, it is also a precursor of the drama of anonymity and revealed identity that would change the course of their lives.

The song itself is not exactly subtle, but subtlety was never part of the Pussy Riot aesthetic. Entitled "Kill the Sexist," it reminds the listener how tired she is of cleaning men's dirty socks, of her mother's dismal toil in her domestic prison, before addressing imagined male interlocutors: "Sniff your own socks/ And don't forget to scratch your ass." They continue:

Burp, spit, booze, shit,
While we'll joyfully be lesbians!
Envy your own penises, suckers,
The long penis of your drinking buddy,
The long penis of the boob tube,
Until the level of shit reaches the ceiling!
Become a feminist, become a feminist,
Peace to the world, and an end to men,
Become a feminist, destroy the sexist,
Kill the sexist, wipe off his blood![2]

To the extent that this song has shock value, it is due largely to its vehemence: the Russian music scene, not to mention Russia in general, had made little room for the expressions of young women's anger (old women, who are expected to berate the young for their flaws, are another matter). The invocation of violence (a rhetorical flourish rather than an actual political program), the references to male genitalia—all of this announced a performative feminism that, while seeming to embrace the man-hating stereotype commonly held by anti-feminists, would soon find a power in barely needing to mention men at all.

Once they decided to actually become the group that they renamed "Pussy Riot," they were joined by several anonymous women (with Petya helping with the logistics) and set out to make their first video in October 2011. As Gessen describes it, the making of "Free the Cobblestones" was as disruptive and chaotic as the video itself, with several tense interactions with the police during the fifteen days of shooting.[3] "Free the Cobblestones" establishes Pussy Riot as culture heroes: when they stand on top of a bus, or on a platform in the metro, the camera pays as much attention to their audience as to them: to the smiling young viewers cheering them on, to the *babushki* complaining about all the nonsense, and, most amusingly, to the undercover members of the anti-extremist task force ("Center E") identified by helpful, scribbled labels pointed at their faces.

The lyrics of "Free the Cobblestone" make a crucial transition, continuing the feminist bravado of "Kill the Sexist" but putting their gender politics in a broader revolutionary, anti-Putinist context, with references to Tahir Square in Egypt (the Arab Spring was still a going, and optimistic, concern) and Libya (the overthrow of Qadafi). Feminism will not just liberate women, it will save Russia: "The Feminist whip is good for Russia!" one of them sings, while brandishing a (presumably feminist) whip. Should anyone doubt the extent of Pussy Riot's political program, the video's release on November 7 (the anniversary of the October Revolution) makes their intentions clear.

Three weeks later, Pussy Riot proved that they were not a one-hit wonder ("Kill the Sexist" hardly counted). "Kropotkin Vodka" (named after the famous Russian anarchist and, well, vodka), added consumerism to their list of targets, with the women bursting into a boutique on the chichi Stoleshnikov Lane. Nadya writes:

> We performed at places where rich Putinists and conformists gather, e.g., on top of Jaguar automobiles, on tables in bars, in shops selling expensive clothing and furs, at fashion shows, cocktail receptions. We performed only one song, because you have time for only one song before you're arrested.[4]

Pussy Riot do their best to disrupt the routines of self-satisfied shoppers. In resisting the culture of commodification, the performers also refuse to commodify themselves. Rarely in the center of a well-composed frame, their bodies are too much in motion to be contained on the screen. In fact, one of the most jarring images comes early, when the camera, almost as if by accident, zeroes in on one of the women's behinds. This brief moment is a reminder of what the video does not do: objectify, sexualize, and chop up the female body for the male gaze.

The song itself took up the theme of domestic drudgery right where "Free the Cobblestone" left off, once again invoking feminism as the path to Russian revolution (even the whip makes another appearance, although this time it isn't mentioned by name). The chorus says it all, though it says it slightly differently each with each repetition: "The fucking sexist conformists are fucked"; "The fucking informant bosses are fucked"; "The fucking sexist Putinists are fucked". As much an incantation as a song, "Kropotkin Vodka" prefigures the Punk Prayer in that it is an exercise in avant-garde political magical thinking, a cry out to the audience to make their words come true.

Just a few days later, Pussy Riot's next performance had a much more specific political agenda. Standing on the roof opposite the facility holding people who had been arrested for protesting the December 2011 state Duma elections, Pussy Riot sang "Death to Prison, Freedom for Protest," to the enthusiastic applause of their (literal) captive audience. This was a general call to rise up against the authorities, using the language of political activism ("Direct action is the future of humanity"). The song starts with a double helping of Nietzsche that invokes his language while undermining his master/slave hierarchy ("The gay science of occupying squares / The will to power without whorish leaders"). "Death to Prison" also appropriates the language of patriotism, but does not cast the usual suspects in the role of savior: "LGBT, feminists, defend the fatherland!"

The political content of all these songs is obvious, but it is worth noting because of the context of the subsequent trial, when the judge refuses any interpretation of the Punk Prayer as being anti-Putinist rather than anti-Orthodox. Nadya would later explain that "when we say 'Putin,' we have in mind the entire bureaucratic machinery that was [...] built by him with the help of the systematic changes in laws, the changes made to the Constitution, ideology, the educational system, and the legal system."[5] But whether they mean the man or the system, Pussy Riot's body of work up through and including the Punk Prayer made Putin its prime target.

Which brings us to their last performance and video before the one that would lead to their arrest: "Putin Pissed Himself."[6] Nadya's point about Putin and the system is well taken, but this time the title sounds decidedly personal (political systems rarely wet their own pants). And yet most of the lyrics are about the system, not the man: "Dissatisfaction with the culture of male hysteria / The wild cult of the leader eats up people's brains." The song was performed and recorded in the heart of Red Square, on Lobnoe Mesto, the circular platform associated in the popular consciousness with public executions. It was their most brazen reclamation of public space from the state thus far.

The song also marks a step towards the Punk Prayer. Not only does Pussy Riot lament the "Orthodox religion of the stiff penis," they call on the most potent female figures in Christianity to join their cause: "The Madonna in glory will learn to fight / The feminist Magdalene is off to a demonstration." With the benefit of the hindsight, "Putin Pissed Himself" looks like the Punk Prayer's rough draft.

# CHAPTER 3
# WHEN IS A CHURCH NOT
# A CHURCH?

The problem faced by the Punk Prayer was Pussy Riot's choice of location. One might think nothing could top a performance on Red Square for sheer gall, but the Cathedral of Christ the Savior proved to be far more fraught—and more controversial—than the members of Pussy Riot expected. In selecting the cathedral, Pussy Riot was continuing its assault on Putinism, this time with special attention to the role of the Russian Orthodox Church in maintaining the current system.

The choice of venue was not just provocative; it was divisive. The standard liberal response to Pussy Riot's notorious "punk prayer" in the cathedral tried to split the difference, amounting to something along the lines of "Of course, I don't approve of doing something like that in a church, but their punishment is unjust." This is the familiar civil libertarian stance that supports a right to do the outrageous while keeping the perpetrators at a safe distance. But this approach misses the point: it is precisely the Cathedral of Christ the Savior as a venue that justifies Pussy Riot's action.

This is because the cathedral itself is the incarnation of scandal; in its designs, redesigns, demolitions and reconstructions, it is not just an appropriate site for conceptual art—it is conceptual art performed in extremely slow motion; it is not just a site of scandal, to many it is itself a scandal. Thus the Cathedral of Christ the Savior is the material foundation of the cultural logic of Pussy Riot.

For a cultural landmark that has been so prominent in the international news, Moscow's Cathedral of Christ the Savior is a strangely unstable site. Indeed, despite the countless tons of stone utilized in its (re)construction, the cathedral has an uncanny tendency to vanish, as if it were an architectural illustration of Jean Piaget's notion of object impermanence—like a child playing peekaboo, how do we know it's still there when we can't see it? The cathedral is culturally significant precisely as the physical manifestation of disappearance, the materialization of the threat of dematerializing. The cathedral recalls the Soviet-era practice of editing the past through doctoring photographs, as shown in David King's 1997 *The Commissar Vanishes: The Falsification of Photographs and Art in Stalin's Russia*. The cathedral, by encompassing a pre-Soviet pre-history, a Soviet demolition, and a post-Soviet reconstruction widens this concept of historical instability, allowing it to span over a century of Russian culture.

In its initial conception, the Cathedral of Christ the Savior was to be the synthesis of Russia's national and spiritual destinies—a commemoration of Moscow's survival in the face of the Napoleonic invasion in 1812. Initially a neoclassical project chock-full of Masonic symbolism, the cathedral was redesigned under Nicholas I in the Russian Revival style (Haskins, 2009). Consecrated in 1883, it was desecrated in 1930—first it was stripped of its gold, and, finally, on 5 December 1931, dynamited by Stalin's government in a public spectacle. Even as the religious basis for the cathedral's importance was negated by official Soviet atheism, its status as a (secular) sacred site was only bolstered by the plans to replace it with the Palace of Soviets, a grandiose Bolshevik Tower of Babel with an enormous statue of Lenin at its summit, like an abandoned groom on top of a Stalinist wedding cake.[1]

The planning and construction of this giant was fraught with problems and eventually interrupted by the outbreak of World War Two. Its frame was, like the gold of its predecessor, cannibalized for more practical use. It was transformed into the immense inversion of its original design: instead of a tower with one person on top, it would become the world's largest open-air pool, with thousands of people bathing at a given time (an unintentional, secular parody of the mass baptism of the Kievan Rus in the Dniepr River in 988). In the late 1990s, the cathedral was reconstructed, initially intended as a near-exact replica but eventually revised due to the input of the reliably tacky architect Zurab Tsereteli.[2]

Every structure on the site is part of an architectural palimpsest of state power and the sacred. Even at a single moment in time, the cathedral/pool exists as a snapshot in an imaginary time-lapse photograph; one imagines a Duchamp pastiche, Cathedral Descending a Staircase. The pool is more than a pool, because its very existence reinforces the desecration of the vanished cathedral. The rebuilt cathedral is either the triumph of a resurgent, state-forming Orthodoxy or the site of a near-criminal disregard for the separation of church and state (not to mention a stark rejection of over 100 years of modern architecture). In that regard, the current building can be seen as the synthesis of a series of church/state alternations: the cathedral has fulfilled its destiny as an entity of both church and state, sanctifying the state in the eyes of hardliners, or profaning the church in the eyes of sceptics.

Before a site was chosen for the Palace of Soviets, Bolshevik leader Sergei Kirov proposed that it be built "on the sites of palaces once owned by bankers, landlords and tsars."[3] The selection of the cathedral's former location would appear to contradict Kirov's idea; the Russian Orthodox Church was strangely absent from this list. But the new cathedral embodies Kirov's hopes perfectly, albeit for ideologically unfriendly purposes. The addition of a business center to the church compound (seen by insiders as separated by a secular firewall, and as outsiders as part of a seamless whole), the availability of parking, and the discrete charms of a gift shop are particularly jarring within the Eastern Orthodox context. American Protestants and Reform Jews are accustomed to seeing their places of worship as multi-purpose rooms, used for AA meetings, clubs, and other activities when no service is going on, while Temple Gift Shops have been supplying a steady stream of kitschy Judaica to generations of Bar and Bat Mitzvahs. The Orthodox Church, however, is traditionally a place of holy mystery, not a part-time community center. Add in the complex finances of the cathedral's reconstruction (with the direct involvement of former Moscow mayor Yuri Luzhkov), and we clearly have a building that is both more and less than a cathedral.[4]

The Cathedral of Christ the Savior is "haunted" by the ghosts of the past, and more specifically, by the ghosts of architecture either razed or left unbuilt. The donation boxes scattered throughout Moscow in the 1990s were usually accompanied by images of the demolished cathedral, functioning as both an advertisement for the future and a memorial for a departed loved one.

Haunted sites in the US are often those that signify a violation through the redefinition of use: churches repurposed as stores or homes, or the proverbial Indian burial ground paved over to make way for a suburban gated community. That is, haunting results from retasking, multitasking, and desecrating a pre-industrial site saturated with meaning. The Cathedral of Christ the Savior is tantamount to taking an Indian burial ground, building a shopping mall on top of it, and then knocking down the shopping mall in order to replace it with a sparkling new Indian burial ground—with a casino attached. From this perspective, the Cathedral of Christ the Savior is a haunted house story just waiting for the ghosts to arrive.

And arrive they did. Singing a scandalous tune.

# CHAPTER 4
## LIKE A (PUNK) PRAYER

The Cathedral of Christ the Savior was many things—too many things, really. But it was not a hospitable setting for shooting a subversive punk feminist music video. When planning the event, the women realized that they were not likely to have much time before being chased away, so they practiced (and recorded) in a similar church on the outskirts of town in order to splice together enough material to give the impression of a complete performance. The raw footage from the cathedral lasts only 1 minute and 34 seconds, little of which was actually used. Most of what we see and hear in the video did not come from that day. If you haven't watched the video recently, go look it up on line, and come back to this book two minutes later.

Since the most scandalous criminal case of 2012 hinged on this performance, a close examination of this video is warranted. If we watch Pussy Riot's videos in order (admittedly, a rather pedantic approach to punk performance art), we immediately see a difference in the shooting style. Though their antics in the subway, on trains, and in Red Square had to be carefully arranged in order to escape excessive police attention, the camerawork on the earlier videos is still fairly steady. "Punk Prayer," by contrast, contains footage that is clearly shot in suboptimal conditions: the camerawork is occasionally shaky, and the camera operator didn't have the chance to frame the women properly (the clearest shots of Pussy Riot come from the B roll taken at the other church). This is not to say that the video is amateurish; a comparison of the finished product with the raw footage (also available on line) shows how well the images were cleaned up. But the overall effect is still, quite appropriately, a bit frantic, if not to say gonzo.

The video is a deliberate study in contrasts: the energetic dancing of the four women in the front of the church alternates with shots of them bowing and crossing themselves (not quite correctly) in a posture of prayer.[1] And, though the security guards who are trying to stop them do get screen time, the video appears much more interested in the green-uniformed female church worker who keeps trying to shoo the camera man out. When we add in the older women watching in disgust, who look like they were answering a casting call for "disapproving, middle-aged Soviet-style women," the "Punk Prayer" to the Mother of God finds definite visual pleasure in juxtaposing such different incarnations of Russian femininity.

The dancing would get Pussy Riot in trouble in court, but it was their words that were equally scandalous. The song is short, and worth examining in its entirety:

(Choir)
Mother of God, Virgin Mary, Cast Putin out,
Cast Putin out, Cast Putin out

Black cassock, golden epaulettes
The whole congregation crawls on its knees
The specter of freedom in the heavens
Gay Pride sent off to Siberia in shackles
The KGB head, their main saint
escorts protesters to jail
So as not to offend His Holiness
Women have to make babies and love
Shit, shit, Holy shit
Shit, shit, Holy shit

(Choir)
Mother of God, Virgin Mary, become a feminist
Become a feminist, become a feminist

The church praises rotten strongmen
Black limos for the Stations of the Cross
A preacher is coming to your school today
Go to class and bring him money!
Gundyai the Patriarch believes in Putin
The bitch should believe in God instead

The Virgin's Belt won't replace demonstrations
The Virgin Mary's joined our protests!

(Choir)
Mother of God, Virgin Mary, Cast Putin out,
Cast Putin out, Cast Putin out

The three choir sections are fairly straightforward, performed in a pseudo-liturgical manner. Mary, the intercessor often called upon for help, is asked to do things: cast Putin out, and become a feminist. The first is consistent with the political aims of Pussy Riot's previous songs, though the wording (which I have tried to preserve) moves Putin from the familiar political arena to that of the demonic. The verb usually used regarding demons (izgnat') has a different prefix from the one used here (prognat'), but they are calling on the Mother of God while standing in a church. The verb isn't exactly accurate, but neither is their performance. More to the point, neither is the church itself; it is supposed to be a house of God, but the Patriarch has used it to stump for Putin. The Punk Prayer is both a set of political demands in the form of a prayer, and a plea for an exorcism in the realm of politics.

Asking Mary to become a feminist is a similar confusion of genres; setting aside the question of ideological content, the words "feminist" and "Mother of God" belong to different semantic realms. Pussy Riot, as usual, is impatient with boundaries and contradictions, and has framed their punk agenda as a holy mission, even as they know that they are the ones who are going to be chased out of the church.

The first verse of the song, by contrast, highlights a boundary crossing of which they disapprove: the historical ties between the Russian Orthodox Church (ROC) and the state secret services. In the early years of the Soviet Union, ROC priests were often persecuted and imprisoned; subsequently, the ROC hierarchy was riddled with KGB agents. In 1992, dissident priest Gleb Yakunin published archival documents demonstrating the Church's close ties to state security, as well as then-Patriarch Alexii II's KGB code name. Nikolai Gundyaev, now Patriarch Kirill of Moscow and all Rus, is commonly assumed by liberal critics to have held similar ties.[2] This would bring him closer to

Putin, himself a former intelligence officer. The Patriarch's black cassock, then, is a poor cover for his KGB epaulettes.

The rest of the verse is both descriptive and prophetic, with references to jailing protesters, banning Gay Pride marches, and anti-feminist, pro-natalist policies. All of these phenomena were visible in the culture at the time of Pussy Riot's performance, and all of them intensified during Putin's third term, when the president's administration put its weight behind the politics of "traditional morality."

The last two lines of the verse were far more shocking than English speakers might suspect: "Shit, shit. Holy shit. / Shit, shit. Holy shit." This phrase, suggested to Pussy Riot by Katya's father, is not part of standard Russian obscene vocabulary, although it did appear now and then before the Punk Prayer. The consensus is that it comes from a literal translation of the English exclamation in American films. In any case, not everyone knows it; during the trial, linguists were called in to discuss whether this was simply slang or blasphemy.[3] It did not help that the Russian phrase actually is more closely linked to God than the American original: literally, it means "The Lord's shit."

The second verse addresses the substance of Pussy Riot's dispute with the ROC: the Patriarch's endorsement of Putin during the presidential campaign and the Church's growing influence over secular institutions. The Virgin's Belt is a holy relic that had been on display in the Cathedral of Christ the Savior, drawing huge crowds in 2011.[4]

Overall, the lyrics of the Punk Prayer are a clever and even, in their own way, almost subtle response to the political and social situation as Pussy Riot saw it. The ROC was trying to assert the primacy of Orthodoxy in what is technically a secular state; the state apparatus was capitalizing on pro-Orthodox sentiments to shore up its own popular support. A concerned skeptic might worry that the church was becoming the state, and the state, the church. The Patriarch, meanwhile, publicly declared Putin's twelve years in power a "miracle from God," denouncing the opposition's criticism as "ear-piercing shrieks."[5] Pussy Riot turns this dynamic on its head, rendering protest itself into a kind of prayer: literally, in their action in the church, and more broadly, in their plea to the Mother of God to join the demonstrations. The Punk Prayer tells us that the church is no longer acting like a holy institution; where Jesus cast the moneylenders out of the Temple, Pussy Riot wants to cast out the apparatus of state (Putin). True faith, then, is found in conscious, political and artistic action. As for the official structures of the Russian Orthodox Church? All they are doing is peddling holy shit.

# CHAPTER 5
## HURTING BELIEVERS' FEELINGS

The women of Pussy Riot had every reason to believe that, even if they were caught, they would at most be charged with an administrative offense. In that scenario, they would be given a fine, but jail time would be out of the question. Creating a disturbance in a church would be the equivalent of an American misdemeanor. Instead, they were charged with "premeditated hooliganism performed by an organized group of people motivated by religious hatred or hostility," an offense punishable by up to seven years in prison.

One of the many remarkable things about their trial was the focus on religion. With witnesses calling their dancing "Satanic," the trial in Khamovniki District Court was a strange cross between a Soviet-era prosecution of dissidents and an amateur production of *The Crucible*. The Russian Federation is, technically, a secular state, but the substance of the accusations against Pussy Riot was essentially about blasphemy.

Blasphemy is a religious offense rather than a legal infraction, so the prosecution focused on the effect the performance allegedly had on the people who became its involuntary audience. One lesson that the state clearly learned from the Pussy Riot trial was that the country needed a stronger legal basis on which to prosecute offenses such as the Punk Prayer. In 2013, Putin signed a law against "public actions" that offend religious sensibilities. The phrase used in the law is often translated as "insulting believers' religious feelings," but it could just as accurately be rendered as "hurting believers' religious feelings." For years, the Russian media had been having a field day over allegations of American "political correctness," and now the country made it illegal to hurt a protected group's feelings.[1] The puns about "harsh Russian winters" and "delicate snowflakes" practically write themselves.

If Pussy Riot as a movement refused to let themselves be pigeonholed by rejecting the boundaries between art, politics, protest, and prayer, their trial turned them into victims of their own success. That is, by operating in so many different spheres at once, they were vulnerable to charges on the grounds of any one of them. Just as American lawyers engage in "judge shopping" (filing lawsuits until they find a judge who will look favorably on their position), the Russian legal system had multiple options to choose from when it came to characterizing Pussy Riot's alleged "crime." Artistic critique was unlikely to get them anywhere, leaving them a choice between politics and religion as the grounds for prosecution. Pussy Riot saw its incursion into the Cathedral of Christ the Savior as a political protest taking the form of a prayer in the venue of a church, with this venue being particularly appropriate for venting their anger at the broken boundaries between church and state. The state had nothing to gain from characterizing Pussy Riot's offense as political, while Pussy Riot could only lose when the performance was framed as an offense to religious believers. Thus every time the lawyers or defendants tried to bring up Putin, the judge told them that Putin and political dissent had nothing to do with the case at hand.

Instead, they were repeatedly questioned about their religious beliefs: Do they consider themselves Orthodox? Do they pray? Do they take communion? The women typically gave complex, nuanced answers to these rather blunt questions (believing in a higher power, or some of the "better" traditions of the Russian Orthodox Church), fighting in vain against an attempt to paint them as radical atheists hell-bent on undermining Orthodoxy. Instead, they made clear that they took issue not with the religion of Orthodoxy, but with church hierarchy, a distinction to which the court was resolutely indifferent. As a result, Pussy Riot's defenders could easily view them as part of a long tradition of persecuted reformers, or even as the defenders of a faith corrupted by greed and political expediency.

In fact, though the media unrelentingly drove home the message that Pussy Riot was the enemy of Orthodoxy, a number of Orthodox voices were raised in their support. As Elena Gapova notes, the women of Pussy Riot, while clearly disaffected from the ROC as an institution, could be seen as part of what the philosopher Mikhail Epstein called "minimal religion," a "phenomenon of post-atheist religiosity" that, rather than concerned with "dogma or ritual can be identified only as an internal impulse, a state of spirit, or a disposition of mind."[2]

Consider the rhetorical question often lobbed their way: what would have happened if Pussy Riot had tried something like this in a mosque? The obvious intent here is to frame any Orthodox or state reaction as "merciful" or "civilized" in comparison to a "fanatical" Islam that would call for their beheading. It might also suggest that the ROC is being unfairly singled out, since other religious institutions are even more illiberal or anti-feminist. Yet the answer to this question is clear, both on the face of it and based on the statements made by the defendants in court: as Slavic citizens of the Russian Federation, they are not implicated in Islam, responsible for it or to it; Islam does not claim to speak in their names. Indeed, this fits with the constant rhetoric about the ROC's "state-forming" role, and its immovable place in Russian culture regardless of faith. Even if we posit that some of the women of Pussy Riot are atheists polemicizing against faith, the God with whom they are arguing is Russian Orthodox.

The three defendants are also frequently castigated for failure to show proper repentance, and here we see a real impasse. At various times, each of them actually said that they had not intended to hurt believers' feelings, and that they were sorry if anyone took offense. But their apologies (which were rarely featured in Russian media coverage) were offered in a spirit of civil, even secular discourse, while the repentance often demanded of them was Orthodox Christian and, ironically, theatrical. Their critics wanted tearful demonstrations of remorse, complete with bowing to and perhaps even embracing the Russian Orthodox Church. Among the suggestions made were that they should be whipped and sent to a convent. Anya Bernstein persuasively argues that the Russian media was preoccupied with punishing the women's bodies, which is certainly true.[3] But they would also only accept an apology that fit into a familiar narrative (like Raskolnikov's bowing to kiss the earth before (spoiler alert) turning himself in at the end of *Crime and Punishment*). Once again, Pussy Riot and the state-mediated audience found no common ground. Their apology, like their Punk Prayer, was a performance that got unfairly harsh reviews.

There is still one more way in which the Punk Prayer can be assimilated into Orthodox theology, if not Orthodox practice, and that involves the idea of the *iurodivyi*, the "holy fool" or the "fool for Christ." While this idea is shared by both Eastern and Western Christianity, it is particularly important for Orthodoxy.[4] To the secular eye, a holy fool looks like the jester in Shakespearean drama (not to mention the fool in Pushkin's *Boris Godunov*), who, precisely because he is a "fool," sees the truth behind facades—a truth that he is not afraid to voice in public. As Sergey A. Ivanov puts it in *Holy Fools in Byzantium and Beyond*, the fool engages in the outrageous behavior of the mad without actually being insane:

> The Orthodox Church holds that the holy fool voluntarily takes upon himself the mask of insanity in order that he may thereby conceal his own perfection from the world and hence avoid the vanity of worldly praise. A further stimulus to such behavior, in the Orthodox view, may be as a comical, paradoxical form of spiritual instruction. However, the holy fool's indecorous behavior can be edifying only if he abandons his disguise (for otherwise how would one tell him apart from a real, non-pretend fool or delinquent?); yet if he does reveal himself, the holy fool subverts his own vocation.[5]

In other words, identifying the holy fool involves questions of intent and performativity: something about the fool's behavior must appear mad while also suggesting that the madness is fake (a deception that becomes clearer precisely when the fool's words or deeds turn out to have revealed the truth). Ivanov uses the word "disguise" here figuratively, yet we cannot help but note how apt the term is for the balaclavas of Pussy Riot.

Thus where the witnesses saw Pussy Riot's dancing as "demonic," possibly a sign of possession, if we view them as holy fools, it proves to be exactly what it so obviously is: a performance. For the case of Pussy Riot, I would rather transpose the dynamic of false madness/revealed truth to that of two stylistic registers: punk provocation and serious speech. After their arrest, the women of Pussy Riot are forced to abandon their more "indecorous behavior" in favor of clear and persuasive language. This was not Pussy Riot's preferred mode of address, but the actions of the state, in unmasking and prosecuting them, obliged them to remove the mask of punk and put on the guise of the rational dissident.

Pussy Riot's critique of the ROC is fundamentally the same as its objection to Putinism, and it is a critique that depends as much on form as it does on substance. Politically, Pussy Riot oppose rigid, undemocratic systems that demand conformity, foster sexism and homophobia, and recast dissent as either disloyalty or blasphemy. If the court system refuses to see the Punk Prayer as targeting both the ROC and the government, they are tacitly ignoring the fundamental argument that the two systems have become too intertwined. As for the form that Pussy Riot chose: it is tenuously consistent with the very idea of church worship (they are performing a prayer), but, more to the point, punk performance refuses to legitimize the systems it opposes by adopting the systems' own language in its entirety. Their holy foolishness is punk foolishness, in that it attacks nonsense posing as truth with truth posing as nonsense.

Aesthetically, this is a clever tactic. Legally, however, it would not serve Pussy Riot well. In court, they would have to find a new language.

# CHAPTER 6
## PUSSY RIOT AND POLITICAL SPEECH

In the best traditions of punk, Pussy Riot excels in the art of rejection and negation; we remember the Sex Pistols and Dead Kennedys for what they condemn ("Nazi Punks—Fuck Off!") far more than for what they celebrate. But Pussy Riot's performances function equally well within the broader realm of Russian political speech, serving as only the most dramatic example of Russian attempts to say no to a prevailing discourse of power. Casual observers of the Russian scene might find a rhetoric of negation unsurprising; the most basic cross-cultural stereotypes would not suggest that citizens of the Russian Federation have difficulty making negative statements. Encounters with public institutions and bureaucracies can reliably produce "no" for an answer to nearly any given question, while more serious studies of Russian speech genres and communications, such as Nancy Ries's *Russian Talk*, have suggested that pessimistic and negative verbal narratives are something of a national art form.[1]

But expressing concerned, public dissatisfaction with the authorities is a much more vexed question. The proximal context for comparison here is, of course, the experience of dissidence in the Soviet Union (and, by extension, throughout the Soviet-led Warsaw Pact alliance). Dissent was indisputably an act of bravery, punishable by intimidation, imprisonment, and exile. The high stakes, combined with the high-minded traditions of the Russian intelligentsia, made dissent an endeavor of high seriousness. Indeed, if Alexei Yurchak's work can be seen as a guide here, low-level dissenters could be perceived as tedious killjoys ("Can't we just vote yes to the latest stupid Komsomol resolution and go out drinking now?").[2] The rhetoric of dissent in the USSR was primarily about truth and justice ("*pravda*"), and thereby resonated with free-thinkers throughout the world (think of Czech dissident playwright Vaclav Havel's "living in truth," or the American leftist ideal of "speaking truth to power").[3] Soviet dissidents were not complete strangers to irony, but their irony was largely unidirectional: it tended to focus on the system.

In their performances (but not, it would turn out, in their courtroom speeches), Pussy Riot dispensed with the declamatory and expository style of Soviet dissent, turning to the parallel traditions of the avant-garde, situationism, Actionism, and conceptual art. These traditions are irony-rich, but content-poor. That is, they express their critique obliquely, tangentially, and often deliberately repulsively. This is certainly the case with "Voina," whose genealogical connections with Pussy Riot are described in Chapter 1. Their antics were nearly always outrageous, and thus referring to their actions in the same breath as those of Pussy Riot became a kind of shorthand for offensiveness (chickens smuggled out of stores in vaginas, orgies in museums). Actionists like Voina and Pussy Riot make political statements without elaborating their actual politics; instead, they draw attention to their political aims through shock and novelty. Elena Volkova and Irina Karatsuba, the two religious scholars detained for wearing balaclavas at the Cathedral of Christ the Savior on the anniversary of the punk prayer, explained their sympathy for Pussy Riot precisely in terms of attention: we had been saying the same thing for years, they said, but no one listened to us.[4]

In its actions, Pussy Riot implicitly recognizes the limited utility of fighting against the regime in the same discursive register as the regime. In this, they differ starkly from dissidents, whose anti-Soviet critiques from the outside seemed to share so many of the premises of Soviet discourse.[5] And it is also consistent not only with the long tradition of Russian absurdism (from the avant-garde Oberiu in the 1920s to the charming and peaceful slacker antics of the Leningrad *Mit'ki* in the 1970s and 1980s), but also with the ethos of the street protests that were taking place at the same time as Pussy Riot's rise to prominence.[6] Recall the playful irony of so many of the signs carried by the protesters—far from the manifestos and open letters of the Brezhnev era, these protests strikingly resembled Facebook status updates, but done in the real world and conveyed by living, human bodies. From dissidence through perestroika, resistance manifested itself most clearly in the direct, unvarnished expression of what was perceived to be long-repressed truth. Today's resistance, of which Pussy Riot is the most spectacular and striking example, is not about glasnost. It is about attracting the scarcest and most desirable resource of the postmodern mediascape: people's attention.

When the three Pussy Riot defendants were put on trial, there was no doubt that they had succeeded in gaining the world's attention. But what they lost was their voice. Coverage in the Russian Federation was limited and one-sided, while the trial itself was conducted with almost laughable partiality. Again and again, Masha, Katya, and Nadya asked to speak, but their requests fell on almost literally deaf ears (kept in a self-contained glass "fishbowl" throughout the trial, they had difficulty simply hearing what was being said, let alone being heard).

We've already seen that the trial was framed entirely in terms of the offended feelings of religious believers, with no room for Pussy Riot's political intentions. Every attempt to bring in politics and Putin was rejected by the judge. This Kafkaesque single-minded opacity is a familiar feature from authoritarian regimes around the world, not to mention the Soviet Union, but it was the lawyers who made the process surreal. As Gessen argues, the dissident experience of the Soviet Union had yielded a familiar script for this sort of trial: the defendants refuse to accept the legitimacy of the charges and the system, while the lawyers address the technicalities.[7] In the case of Pussy Riot, it was the reverse. The lawyers took every opportunity to speechify and grandstand, while it was left to the defendants to think about how the trial was actually being conducted. Meanwhile, the whole event played out like a farce, and like an ongoing struggle between the Judge and the trial's spectators. As Maksim Hanukai notes in the statements by the translators of Pussy Riot's closing speeches, Judge Marina Syrova was obliged to "remind the audience not to applaud the defendants, for, 'Ladies and gentlemen, we are not at the theater.'"[8] For the defendants, however, this was a difference that made no difference. Yes, their lives were at stake, but, yes, this was also one in a series of absurd public events involving Pussy Riot.

The most concise closing statement was the last one, delivered by Katya. From the beginning, she refuses to see her words as an opportunity to "repent" or "enumerate attenuating circumstances." Instead, she offers a cogent analysis of the current Russian political scene, with particular attention to the role of the Russian Orthodox Church, all serving as background to explaining why Pussy Riot chose the venue that it did. She sees a clear alliance between church and state, which work together to "confront all pernicious manifestations of contemporary mass culture with its concept of diversity and tolerance":

> Our sudden musical appearance in the Cathedral of Christ the Savior [...] violated the integrity of the media image that the authorities had spent such a long time generating and maintaining, and revealed its falsity. In our performance we dared, without the Patriarch's blessing, to unite the visual imagery of Orthodox culture with that of protest culture, thus suggesting that Orthodox culture belongs not only to the Russian Orthodox Church, the Patriarch, and Putin, but that it could also ally itself with civic rebellion and the spirit of protest in Russia.[9]

Katya's statement was short, analytical, and uncompromising, ending in the optimistic spirit of a manifesto: "Compared to the judicial machine, we are nobodies, and we have lost. On the other hand, we have won. The whole world now sees that the criminal case against us has been fabricated." It was an optimism tempered by realism (she admits that the court will inevitably find them guilty), nor was it based on empirical evidence (held in prison, she had no access to any). But it was suitably, and predictably, defiant.

Katya was preceded by Masha, whose speech was longer and somewhat less coherent. She, too, sees the Pussy Riot case as a chance to expose the flaws of the system: "Russia, as a state, has long resembled an organism sick to the core." She condemns her country's educational systems as factories of conformity, and alludes to her own experience in psychiatric institutions in order to condemn them as instruments of oppression. She moves on to her environmental activism, to the lack of "horizontal connections" among Russian citizens, and then to her assertion that the Russian government itself is engaging in its own kind of artless performance. Far more than Katya, she engages with the religious component of the trial, in her case by quoting from the Gospels and asserting that the prosecution itself is religiously illiterate.

Her best moment comes when she attacked the language used in the case against her and her fellow defendants: "what really irritates me is how the prosecution uses the words 'so-called' in reference to contemporary art." She connects the phrase to the persecution of dissidents in Soviet times (when future Nobel laureate Joseph Brodsky was dismissed as a "so-called poet"). Everything Pussy Riot sincerely values is reduced to the realm of the "so-called"; "Our apologies, it seems, are also being defined by the collective prosecuting body as 'so-called' apologies." Insisting that their apologies were sincere, Masha turns the prosecution's language against it:

> But for me this trial is a "so-called" trial. And I am not afraid of you. I am not afraid of falsehood and fictitiousness, of sloppily disguised deception, in the verdict of the so-called court. Because all you can deprive me of is "so-called" freedom. This is the only kind that exists in Russia.

Masha concludes her speech with an earnest intensity that is worlds apart from the aggressive irony of Pussy Riot's performances. With the conviction that would have made a Soviet-era dissident proud, she declares that she "thirst[s] for truth," and that freedom itself will inevitably come.

As usual, it was Nadya who brought the house down. Though all three defendants were intelligent, well-read, and well-spoken, Nadya's closing statement was a showcase for her rhetorical gifts. Foreshadowing the themes to be developed by her comrades, Nadya began by rejecting the very legitimacy of the trial and the courtroom, choosing to put "the entire political system of the Russian Federation" on trial instead. She compares the court apparatus to the infamous "troikas" of the Stalin-era show trials when, as now, the verdicts were a foregone conclusion. From there she gives the closest thing to Pussy Riot's artistic manifesto:

What was behind our performance at the Cathedral of Christ the Savior and the subsequent trial? Nothing other than the autocratic political system. Pussy Riot's performances can either be called dissident art or political action that engages art forms. Either way, our performances are a kind of civic activity amidst the repressions of a corporate political system that directs its power against basic human rights and civil and political liberties. The young people who have been flayed by the systematic eradication of freedoms perpetrated through the aughts have now risen against the state. We were searching for real sincerity and simplicity, and we found these qualities in the yurodstvo [the holy foolishness] of punk.

Just as her arrest and prosecution forcibly unmasked her as the face behind one of the balaclavas, Nadya lays bare the devices behind Pussy Riot's artistry. Punk performance was meant to combat the "rigidity" of the state's hierarchic structures. Politically, the group opposes the coercive mechanisms of state security, "imposed civic passivity," the dominance of the executive branch, and the "scandalous dearth of political culture."

Like Katya, she claims victory for Pussy Riot, as well as widespread support, even among Orthodox believers. But most striking are the claims she makes on behalf of Pussy Riot and herself: they are the forces of sincerity and truth that will "triumph over the paths of cunning, guile, and deception." She constructs a bridge between the provocative lyrics of the Punk Prayer and the more straightforward, declarative language she uses in her speech, by asserting that only those opposing the regime have freedom of expression:

We can say anything we want and we say everything we want. The prosecution can only say what they are permitted to by political censorship. They can't say "punk prayer," "Our Lady, Chase Putin out," they can't utter a single line of our punk prayer that deals with the political system.

Implicitly, this is an argument for a power of performance that extends beyond the instance of performing: the words of the Punk Prayer, and by extension, Nadya's speech, take on an almost magic power, and even repeating them in order to negate them is too dangerous for the regime.

The rest of Nadya's statement elaborates on the power of speech, first by contrasting the actions of a court that charges them with crimes against Christian believers with the words of Christ ("I forgive them"), then showing how words betray those who speak with insincerity (the prosecuting attorney who, in a Freudian slip, called Pussy Riot "the injured party"). She notes that the entire trial has been set up in order to keep the women silent, with the court not allowing them to speak during the initial five months of their incarceration. When they were finally permitted to say something, on July 30, they "called for making contact and facilitating dialogue, not for battle and confrontation." Their overture was rejected, and, most important, their words were rejected as well:

> "You are not sincere," they said to us. Too bad. Do not judge us according to your behavior. We spoke sincerely, as we always do. We said what we thought. We were unbelievably childlike, naive in our truth, but nevertheless we are not sorry for our words, and this includes our words on that day.

Nadya takes up the theme developed by her fellow defendants (that is, that they are freer in prison than most people are at liberty), and goes on to situate their struggle historically, in a decidedly un-punk fashion. First, she invokes Solzhenitsyn, then Alexander Vvedensky, of the avant-garde OBERIU movement in the 1920s, and then moves on to Dostoevsky, Socrates, and Christ. I bring this up not to accuse her of hypocrisy—far from it. After all, one of the main themes elaborated in the present study is Pussy Riot's refusal to be bound by conventional notions of genre or consistency. But Nadya's closing statement is the starkest example of the group's willingness to adapt to circumstances and audience, something that would seem to be the exact opposite of the political aesthetic that drove them to perform in an Orthodox cathedral. For avant-garde artists, their approach to speech and audience proves rather utilitarian: they will avail themselves of whatever speech genres and artistic codes that might be necessary for a given endeavor. This basic fact is crucial for contextualizing Nadya's and Masha's actions once they are freed from imprisonment, opening up a third possibility besides recommitting to avant-garde practice or "selling out." Pussy Riot is not dogmatic; it is not a group of purists demanding the faithful implementation of a political or artistic program. Their best performances were always a compromise between planning and improvisation. And from the moment they were arrested, Katya, Masha, and Nadya were obliged to improvise non-stop.

# CHAPTER 7
# PUBLIC ENEMIES

The Actionists of Pussy Riot had hoped to inspire a new wave of public, political creativity. Their success must be considered qualified. On the plus side, there were a number of public protests in the wake of their arrest that often elaborated on Pussy Riot's provocative aesthetic, as most clearly demonstrated by the work of the performance artist Pyotr Pavlensky.

Where Pussy Riot deployed their brightly clad bodies with a frenzied activity whose "unladylike" character was part of the point, Pavlensky's body remained unmistakably individual, but the artist used it as a kind of voodoo doll in reverse. The real and discursive violence of the state was repeatedly enacted on Pavlensky's painfully vulnerable body. In 2012, in protest of Pussy Riot's imprisonment, Pavlensky sewed his lips shut. The next year, his naked body, wrapped in coils of barbed wire, was placed in front of a St. Petersburg government building. A few months later, Pavlensky was naked once again, this time nailing his scrotum to the stone pavement of Red Square. In 2014, Pavlensky, whom forensic psychiatrists declared sane after each one of his previous arrests, sat naked on the roof of Russia's most notorious mental hospital and cut off one of his earlobes.[1]

The women of Pussy Riot would have a more complicated relationship with a sister organization that supported them during their incarceration: the Ukrainian/international women's collective Femen, best known for topless public protests. When pressed, Nadya and the others disagreed with Femen's tactics, which included publicly chopping down crucifixes. One of the anonymous members of Pussy Riot, who goes by the nickname "Serafima," told a Vice reporter,

> Our opinion on Femen is a complicated story. On one hand, they exploit a very masculine and sexist rhetoric in their protests—men want to see aggressive naked girls attacked by

cops. On the other hand, their energy and the ability to keep on going no matter what, is awesome and inspiring.[2]

For her part, Nadya found Femen to be under-theorized: "Femen has a different ideological basis; for the most part, we are disrupting the "masculine/feminine" binary, while they insist on it. We like fluid, transgressive queer identities."[3]

And as for the real or imagined incidents of church desecration and vandalism reported in the wake of the Pussy Riot trial, none of this was met with a single approving word by the women of the collective.

Pussy Riot may have been an inspiration for its supporters, but for state television, the group was a godsend. The central TV channels had a history of portraying opposition figures in the worst possible light, and Pussy Riot's activities were so far beyond the pale that one might imagine there was little need to distort them for propaganda purposes. As it turned out, however, both the Pussy Riot trial and Pussy Riot's performances would be carefully curated for a national audience to limit any possibility of a sympathetic perspective.

Just as the courtroom allowed the women virtually no possibility to express themselves during the trial, state television did its best to restrict the audience's access to the women's actual words and performances. While it is true that the Pussy Riot clips were widely available on the Internet, one cannot assume that the average television viewer would bother to look for them.

Viewers were treated to updates about Pussy Riot on the evening news over the course of the trial, but the most concerted attempt to put forward an anti-Pussy Riot narrative was made on the weekly television program *Special Correspondent*. *Special Correspondent* had been a fixture of the state-run Channel 1 since 2002, undergoing a change in format not long before the trial. Now hosted by Arkady Mamontov, the show screened medium-length documentaries before a studio audience and panel of experts, with discussion of the issues raised by the film immediately afterwards.

Pussy Riot provided *Special Correspondent* with a wealth of juicy material. So much, in fact, that by the end of 2012, *Special Correspondent* had aired three episodes dedicated to the group, its trial, and its significance for Russia. Entitled *Provocateurs*, *Provocateurs 2*, and *Provocateurs 3*, these episodes dispensed with any pretense of objectivity. Their goal, which Mamontov pursued doggedly, was to show that Pussy Riot was part of a concerted and dangerous Western plot to destroy Russia, both as a state and as a bulwark of true morality.

Whatever the subject matter, Mamontov does his best to define or redefine the terms of the debate in order to lead the audience to the desired conclusion. Not long after the *Provocateurs* trilogy, he made a documentary about the "LGBT menace" entitled "Sodom," the source of a term he insisted on using throughout his show. He refused to use standard terms such as "homosexual" (*gomoseksual*) or even the outmoded "homosexualist" (*gomoseksualist*); the target of his ire was always "Sodomites" (*sodomity*).[4]

In the three Pussy Riot episodes, Mamontov performs a similar lexical trick: he almost always refers to the Pussy Riot women as the "*koshchunnitsy*" (scoffers) and "*bogokhulnitsy*" (blasphemers). This puts anyone defending them in the position of apologizing for blasphemy, while also foreclosing the possibility that their actions might be otherwise construed. Moreover, in the course of a legal case centered around allegations of religious hatred, Mamontov not only reinforces the anti-religious interpretation of the Punk Prayer, he moves it into a domain that the courts technically cannot address, no matter how much the prosecution clearly wants to: blasphemy in a secular state is not a civil crime.

As a producer and director, Mamontov does share one trait with the women he despises: his work is far from subtle. It is not enough to entitle the documentaries "Provocateurs"; he includes a title sequence depicting serpents crawling across the screen and weaving through the title's letters (the serpents occasionally return as a transitional device for scene changes, usually weaving around the Pussy Riot women themselves). In the first film, recordings of the women being interrogated after their arrest (already not the most flattering of video formats) are paused at moments that make them look particularly sinister, and the sound of their laughter is re-run on occasion in the background.[5] Mamontov's work-ethic here is almost admirable; given

Pussy Riot's antics, he could have made them unappealing to a mass viewer with much less effort.

Mamontov sets the stage for the Punk Prayer by first showing surveillance camera footage of the entrance to the cathedral, as ominous music plays in the background. Then we see the face of an innocent, wide-eyed little boy looking reverently at the images on the walls of the church. The narrator informs us that the steps to this church were washed in the blood of the people who gave their lives for country and their faith (a rather grand claim for a cathedral reconstructed with private donations during peace time, but this hardly matters to Mamontov).

The initial film has a set of small goals, which it accomplishes rather easily. The first is to portray Pussy Riot and the Punk Prayer not as an act of political protest, but as the result of unadulterated evil. The devil, the narrator informs us, means "provocateur." Pussy Riot is an amoral, Satanic force (Mamontov repeatedly treats the audience to delicately expurgated images from the Biological Museum orgy). The man responsible for their initial interrogation says the women behaved as if they were under hypnosis, and when Nadya spoke, you could see sparks in her eyes, like those in horror films about demonic possession.

The second goal is to equate an attack on the Russian Orthodox Church with the desire to destroy Russia "as a nation." In keeping with the Putin-era media's constant emphasis on the ROC as a "state-building" institution, the film and the experts in the audience repeatedly remind us of the holiness of Russia and the primacy of the church: "They are attacking the holy of holies"; "A nation that doesn't have respect for itself won't be a nation for very long"; "We'll stop being a people . . . they want to strip of us of our historical and spiritual bearings."[6]

The largest goal is the one that would be the main focus of the subsequent "Provocateurs" episodes: explaining why the Pussy Riot affair happened and ferreting out the hidden guilty parties responsible for this attack on Russian spirituality and statehood.

Episode 2 poses the central question: Was this just petty hooliganism? Or was it an act of war against the Russian Orthodox

Church? Obviously, the answer has to be war. Mamontov and his experts begin to lay out a set of conspiracy theories that explain the Pussy Riot phenomenon. A "serious" team must be behind Pussy Riot, with "serious money." They are part of a plot try to keep church and state separate, and part of a decades-long assault on Christianity.[7]

Mamontov and his guests oscillate between describing Pussy Riot as puppets and condemning them as revolutionaries. Calling them revolutionaries is important because, as one of the experts notes, "The first revolutionary was Satan." But they are also framed within a conspiracy theory that relies less on Biblical texts, and more on the American Right: echoing Fox News's warnings about "cultural Marxism," one of the experts connects Pussy Riot to the Frankfurt School, which he said combined communism and Freudianism in order to bring the world to ruin.

The rest of the episode is primarily devoted to Pussy Riot's alleged pernicious influence and to their support in the West. A journalist interviews two young men who defaced a provincial church (basically because it seemed like a cool thing to do), only to find God, repent, and join the congregation they had offended. Mamontov also links Pussy Riot to Femen and its cross-destroying actions, despite Pussy Riot's own rejection of such tactics (images of the topless activists cutting down a cross are interspersed with footage of Nadya laughing demonically).

The third and final episode, which aired after the women were sentenced, serves primarily to answer the question raised repeatedly during the previous two: who is behind this? At no point does anyone involved in *Special Correspondent* seriously entertain the idea that Pussy Riot is exactly what it purports to be: an anonymous, non-hierarchical actionist collective composed entirely of women. The reasons for this reflexive skepticism are twofold.

First, and most obviously, there is elementary sexism. The idea that a bunch of "girls" might be interested in these sorts of activities, let alone plan and conduct them on their own, appears inconceivable. None of the names or parties who are alleged to be "behind" Pussy Riot are female, though one could see this as the predictable consequence of Russia's primarily male rogue's gallery of alleged enemies. Nor is it only men who have difficulty imagining committed political activism on the part of women. During an interview with Katya, Ksenia Sobchak, the former party-girl turned opposition journalist, expressed shock at the idea that "girls" might get together to talk about sexism, rather than about guys, shopping, and parties.[8]

The second reason for the constant denigration of Pussy Riot as independent actors must be understood within the context of the state and state media's persistently conspiratorial framing of all independent political activity. Legitimate politics is the purview of the state apparatus and the government-affiliated parties (particularly United Russia). Every time there is a street protest, public demonstration, or online campaign, commentators inevitably insinuate that the opposition is being directed and funded by the usual suspects: disgraced oligarchs, George Soros, and the US State Department.[9]

In Pussy Riot's case, all of these ne'er-do-wells get name checked, in Mamontov's documentary and elsewhere. Right-wing ideologue Alexander Prokhanov, a panelist at the screening of *Provocateurs 3*, puts the case in no uncertain terms. There is a liberal "machine" in Russia and abroad that is trying to break down the walls of the Kremlin and demonize the Russian Orthodox Church. "This operation was planned by these strategists of contemporary liberalism," with no expense spared.[10]

The key figure common to so many of these conspiracy theories is Pyotr (Petya) Verilov. Mamontov and his panelists continually remind the audience of Petya's Canadian passport, claiming that Nadya has one as well. The third documentary keeps returning to still images from the American tour made by him and the first team of Pussy Riot lawyers, noting at one point that Petya "didn't need a visa" to come to the United States. The producers also make sure to show footage of Petya's and Nadya's young daughter Gera on the tour, looking tired, bored, or angry.

Petya's acceptance of an award from Yoko Ono draws the wrath of the panelists, and also sparks a surprisingly poignant complaint from one of them: he feels betrayed that the idols of his youth (the surviving Beatles and their families) support this anti-Russian campaign.

Meanwhile, panelist Iosif Prigozhin says outright that Petya is "either a recruited saboteur or mentally ill."

Petya is a gift to conspiracy-minded sexists: his past leadership of Voina, his Canadian passport, and his excellent English make him an easy target for allegations of nefarious foreign ties. And his role as Nadya's common-law husband means that he can be portrayed as the man who has masterminded the scandalous activities of the Pussy Riot "girls." Thus two of the fundamental tenets of Pussy Riot are rejected out of hand: the viability of independent, self-directed political action and the power of women working separately from men.

# CHAPTER 8
## PERFORMANCE VS. ARCHIVE

One of the challenges in trying to understand Pussy Riot brings us back to that fundamental feature of the group's project: their radical indeterminacy. Since Pussy Riot refuses to be "just" a band, "just" an Actionist collective, "just" a vehicle for political protest, it is tempting to focus on just the aspects of the Pussy Riot phenomenon of immediate interest, to the detriment of the rest. Pussy Riot came to international attention because of issues related to politics and religion, and so politics and religion have taken up a significant share of this book's real estate.

A book of scholarly non-fiction cannot replicate what Pussy Riot does in its art, performance, and activism: it cannot be all things at once. Or at least, this one can't. Where Pussy Riot is provocative in its boundary crossing and genre mixing, its explicators end up plodding behind them, treating each aspect separately and methodically. But if this book cannot partake of Pussy Riot's aesthetic, it can at least do its best to try to analyze and explain it. Hence the focus of the present chapter: Pussy Riot's work as art, or, more specifically, performance art.

Certainly, Pussy Riot has been understood and accepted by many as performance art, including some of performance art's most prominent practitioners (such as Karen Finley). And just as certainly, Pussy Riot comes out of a Russian performance art tradition that we discussed briefly in Chapter 1. But Pussy Riot is more than just an example of performance art; the group's work helps illuminate some of the most important questions surrounding performance art in the age of the internet and viral video.

Performance art is about presence, embodiment, physicality, and ephemerality, all of which is a fancy way of saying "you had to be there."[1] The fact that we even need mention presence at all indicates just how much our understanding of art has changed in just over a century. Before the advent of the now-common forms of media (film, television, radio, audio recording, and perhaps, if one wants to go back that far, the written word), presence was simply assumed as a prerequisite to performance and its audience: there was no other way to experience art that unfolded over time (that is, not simply static visual images, but sequences of actions or sound). Theater may have had a script, but the script was not the same as the experience. Anyone who has ever read a play before going to see it performed can testify to the fundamental difference between text and event.

Recording changed all that. Or rather, it superseded and circumscribed it. We can never know what any particular acclaimed production of Shakespeare in the nineteenth century was actually like, but anyone can watch Laurence Olivier's Oscar-winning film adaptation of *Hamlet* (1948). For the first few decades after its production, finding the opportunity to view the film might have presented obstacles, but the VCR, DVD, and streaming video now provide instantaneous access. Theater, meanwhile, is not dead, but its role in the artistic and cultural ecosystem is vastly diminished. Video is always available; going to see a play is, pun intended, a production.

Just as the camera freed painting from the need to be representational, video recording, by fixing a sequence of events in a format that can, at least conceivably, be played and replayed forever, helped inspire a new, and different, appreciation of the power of the live. This was by no means the only factor in the rise of performance art, which traces its roots back to the avant-garde movements that began before World War I.[2] But it does establish a tension between the live and the recorded, a tension that many artists, Pussy Riot included, have found productive.

As is so often the case in the Pussy Riot story, the turning point for the relationship between live performance and video is the Punk Prayer. Prior to the event at the Cathedral of Christ the Savior, Pussy Riot appeared to prioritize the live event, even as it produced compelling video as both documentation (archive) and as a means of reaching a much wider audience. The only exception would be their first song, ascribed to "Pisya Riot" and prepared to accompany Katya's and Nadya's presentation on Russian feminist art: "Kill the Sexist." Since "Pisya Riot" did not actually exist (yet), the recording played by

Katya and Nadya was essentially the documentation of a non-existent event, a recording of a performance whose original constituted a fake.

Once they actually formed Pussy Riot, their subsequent songs are as much an excuse to arrange a public action as the action was an occasion to perform the song. Here Pussy Riot was continuing the practices of Voina: carefully selecting a venue, planning their entrance and crafting an escape, and, most important, becoming an event that intervenes in the lives of the random passers-by forced to become their audience. Technically, all of this could have been done without any recording equipment, but the limitations here are obvious: the event remains a part of local folklore rather than a contribution to global performance art. If a punk performs and no one records her, does she make a sound? Or enough of a sound to matter?

When the women of Pussy Riot talk about those early songs that we now know entirely as videos, they are not using the language of video production. Instead, they tell the stories of their narrow escape from the police, the mixed reaction of the audience, and the sudden discovery that the bag of flour they dumped all over the premises of their "Kropotkin Vodka" performance was dangerously flammable.[3] This is not the stuff of DVD commentary for an HBO prestige drama; it's tales from the Actionist front.

But why is this all so important? The "liveness" of Actionist performance is an aesthetic and philosophical statement, but it is also intensely political. By using real public, available space and deploying their own bodies in that space, they render themselves both vulnerable and undeniably present. This is what Pyotr Pavlensky picks up on in his post-Pussy Riot performances (enclosing his naked body in barbed wire, sewing his mouth shut, and mutilating himself in various grotesque fashions), and it is also why street protest is still so crucial in the age of online "slacktivism." It is when human bodies take to the street that the regime has to notice, and has to act. Street protest is a weapon, but, in the face of a powerful state repressive apparatus, it is the weaponization of human physical vulnerability rather than human strength. Taking to the streets is about risking one's body, exposing it to the instruments of police violence; when successful, street protests can marshal outrage from moments of terrible violence and abuse.

When it fails, it means that the abuse or incarceration of the vulnerable body might continue indefinitely, or lead to death.

Even when the agenda is not expressly political, the liveness of performance is often the crucial component of its status as art. Marina Abramović caused an international sensation in the spring of 2010, when she mounted an exhibition called *The Artist Is Present* at the Museum of Modern Art (MOMA) in New York. Both a one-woman show and a performance with a literal cast of thousands, *The Artist Is Present* ran for a total of 736 and a half hours and consisted entirely of Abramović sitting silently at a table, making eye contact with the person sitting across from her. Visitors stood in line for hours at a time in order to get their face time with Abramović.

When we think of the role of technology in the work of Pussy Riot, Abramović's example is instructive. There is, of course, video documentation of parts of the exhibition, but such video only emphasizes the medium's inadequacy. The experience was about unmediated, face-to-face contact between an artist and her viewers. This did not prevent a series of ancillary projects from popping up on the internet, none of which needed Abramović's direct participation or consent. The Tumblr page "Marina Abramović Made Me Cry" does not feature the artist at all; instead, it is a collection of photos of the teary faces of visitors as they sat across from Abramović.[4] The avant-garde game designer Pippin Barr, who specializes in games that force the player to confront boredom, released three Abramović-themed games, including one that requires the player's avatar to wait in lines for hours before sitting across from an avatar of Abramović.[5]

Such online extensions are an ingenious means of leveraging a presence-based, non-technological project in a way that does not require presence at all. At the same time, they remind the viewer or player of the essential importance of the presence which, for them, is always absent. I write this as someone thoroughly impressed by Abramović, but too lazy to take the twenty-minute subway ride to MOMA while her exhibit was open. Recording technology is not the enemy of live performance; it brings the idea of the performance to a much wider audience. But it is no substitute for presence.

Finally, one of the advantages of liveness over the recorded archive has legal repercussions, as is clearly the case with the Punk Prayer. Live performance creates its own context, but recordings can be manipulated and excerpted, taken out of context for purposes hostile to the performance's presumed intent. In the *Provocateurs* films, the producers were able to recycle particularly provocative moments from the Punk Prayer, playing them practically on loop. When creating the Punk Prayer video, Pussy Riot made editorial choices, deciding what to include and what to leave out. The same sort of editorial choices are also made by those who use parts of the Punk Prayer video to push their own agenda.

This is inevitable with any recording. With the Punk Prayer, the stakes were higher, and the artistic project was of a different sort from the group's previous performances. With the earlier songs, one could argue for the priority of the live action over the recording, or for considering the two works to be of equivalent status. The Punk Prayer could not function in the same way. On the one hand, it was vital to the women that they actually make it into the Cathedral of Christ the Savior to play their song. In this case, the location might be deemed of greater importance than the performance's liveness. As we saw in Chapter 3, the cathedral is of huge symbolic and political significance.

On the other hand, they were fully aware in advance that they would not be permitted to mount a complete performance in the cathedral. The decision to film a B roll in a similar church suggests that the live event was not enough for their purposes. Had they been interested in the mere fact of documentation, they could have released the raw video and called it a day. Instead, they combined the two recordings in order to make a video whose success depends primarily on its editing.

As a result, the Punk Prayer is unlike any of Pussy Riot's previous work, because it is a finished project creating the illusion that it documents a live performance. The previous videos were indexical; that is, they pointed to the performance, which they reproduced in edited form for the non-present viewer. The Punk Prayer is a successful video rescued from a failed performance. By "failed" I do not refer to the performance's quality, but to the circumstances that prevented it from lasting long enough to get through the song.

The status of the Punk Prayer, then, is one of unresolved contradictions. As performance art, the Punk Prayer is a copy without an original, a video that tricks its viewer into thinking that a longer, less harried rendition of the song somehow took place. It is the documentation of, if not a non-event, then an aborted one. But when Pussy Riot went on trial, the prosecutors refused to treat the video as what it actually was: an edited, semi-falsified version of the performance in the cathedral. Instead, the video took on the status of evidence. It documented a crime. Though it was the Soviet Union in the 1920s that pioneered the film editing technique known as montage (with the films of Sergei Eisenstein at the vanguard), the trial of Pussy Riot unfolded as if no one in Russia were expected to have heard of editing.

Despite all the hair-splitting of the previous paragraphs, the Punk Prayer was very much an event in Actionist terms, in that it disrupted people's assumptions, expectations, and habits, while being an affront to a certain conservative worldview. If racing to the front of the most controversial cathedral in the nation in order to sing a punk feminist song is not an event, what is? Especially since that event had such powerful real-world consequences, with the women's arrest and conviction being only most obvious among them.

The Pussy Riot trial reminds us that artists have only limited control over the reception of their work. The trial of artists for their work is a genre of its own, especially in Russia, with its rich and sad history of persecuting writers by prosecuting them for their words. In order to treat art as infraction, such trials follow a very basic interpretive strategy: they start out by treating the texts with a thudding literalism, deviating from this path for the sake of obvious ideological interpretations that support the prosecution.

In the 1970s, the American poet and singer Gil Scott-Heron popularized a 1960s Black Power slogan in his song "The Revolution Will Not Be Televised." The idea was that the powers-that-be would never allow the masses to see an actual popular uprising on the channels that brought them trashy sitcoms such as "The Beverly

Hillbillies." Pussy Riot's video would not be shown on state television in its entirety (the authorities had taken the lessons of editing to heart), but by this point, sites such as YouTube had broadened the definition of what "televising" might really mean. Pussy Riot did not start an actual revolution. But the revolution that did not take place was nonetheless televised.

# CHAPTER 9
# GENDER TROUBLES

Out of all the possible scenarios in which anti-government protest were to take off in Putin's Russia, could anyone have expected that this would involve the word "pussy"? This is not just a question of the word's taboo status. As a not-unimportant part of cisgender female anatomy, it stands for a whole set of questions about the status of women. But who would have thought the new Russian revolution would be feminist?

Feminism in Russia has had a long and complicated history; the concept of "gender" has a much shorter one. In the years leading up to the Russian Revolution, the most influential versions of Marxism had long proclaimed that communism would lead to women's emancipation from domestic slavery and her attainment of equal status with men. Women would join men in the labor force, while domestic chores, childrearing included, would become an enterprise of collective labor. After the Revolution, the new Soviet constitution guaranteed women's equality, considerably relaxed the family code, and legalized abortion, homosexuality, and lesbianism. The Communist Party established special organizations for women and women's issues, particularly the Zhenotdel (Women's Section).

From the beginning, Bolshevik feminists had a bit of a messaging problem. Their Marxist belief in the gradual withering away of the family alienated some of the women whose lives they hoped to improve. Despite continued reassurances that public childcare would be entirely voluntary, some women felt that their way of life was under threat. When the Bolshevik Inessa Armand proclaimed the virtues of communal kitchen and nurseries at the 1918 All-Russian Women's Congress, she was met with shouts "We won't give up our children." The most prominent Bolshevik Feminist, Alexandra Kollontai, would later conclude that talk of such policies alienated women from the new regime.[1]

A backlash against the liberal family code grew throughout the 1920s. The prevalence of orphan street children in the aftermath of the civil war made the traditional family unit look much more appealing; the ease with which divorce was now filed left many women abandoned by their husbands, but stuck with the children; the more radical proclamations of a new Bolshevik "free love" were outweighed by a new, revolutionary puritanism; and, perhaps most important, the social service infrastructure that was supposed to allow for the complete transformation of the family materialized in a partial and largely unsatisfactory form. By the time Stalin consolidated power and launched a nationwide industrialization drive in the late 1920s, the appetite for domestic revolution had grown quite small, feminists were marginalized, and the family unit was championed as a basic cell of socialist society. Moreover, the state, concerned about Soviet demographics, pursued pro-natalist policies, outlawing abortion between 1936 and 1955, providing little access to birth control, and encouraging large families (the latter with little success). Male homosexuality became a criminal offense in 1936, and would only be legalized again in 1993, while lesbians lived under the threat of psychiatric hospitalization.[2]

One radical change was accomplished on a massive scale: the near-total inclusion of women in the labor force. However, in the absence of satisfactory national childcare and the failure of industrial-scale communal kitchens to supplant women's traditional domestic duties, women found themselves serving a second shift at home after a full day's work. And here is where we see the "feminism" incorporated into Soviet policy and the waves of postwar Western feminism diverge.

The point of the comparison is not to present the West as a feminist paradise, or to suggest that Western working women did not also bear the burden of the second shift. But there are crucial differences. When feminism was revived in the West, it was a grass-roots movement that was able to call into question a whole range of traditional assumptions. In Soviet times, such a movement was all but impossible. Even more important, Western feminist movements were obliged to develop theories about gender, and to open a dialogue about the distinction between "natural" sex differences and socially constructed (and therefore mutable) gender roles. Western men have been slow to shoulder their share of the second shift's burden, but Soviet men were rarely expected to even think about such inequities.

One of the rare discussions of Soviet gender roles in the 1970s centered on men rather than women. The huge death tolls in World War II resulted in a demographic imbalance between men and women, strengthening a pre-existing trend of children being raised primarily by mother and grandmothers in the absence of male parental figures. The concern raised in pedagogical journals and Soviet newspapers was that men had become "infantilized."[3] Pampered at home by adoring women, unable to realize their "natural" roles as leaders and breadwinners thanks to the strong role of the state, and falling prone to alcoholism at alarming rates, men, rather than women, were considered to be in a precarious situation.

Meanwhile, the few feminist activists and organizations to arise in the late Soviet period were marginalized, with no access to any public forums. With the advent of perestroika and glasnost under Gorbachev in the 1980s, feminists finally gained a public voice, writing articles and books, appearing on talk shows, establishing crisis lines and research organizations. They also imported the term "gender" into Russian, a word that would always sound strange and foreign.

Feminists in the 1980s and 1990s were fighting a difficult battle. The new capitalist economy that started to develop in the 1980s (only to take off for real in the 1990s) was dominated by men. Moreover, that domination was largely accepted as a given: finally, formally infantilized former Soviet men had the opportunity to make something of themselves. As for (post-)Soviet women, rather than see the new system as an opportunity to redefine gender roles in a more equitable fashion, many of them seemed to welcome the possibility that having a successful husband could free them from having to work outside the home. That is, rather than divide up the second shift, some opted to give up the first. According to some polls, prostitution, which technically did not exist in Soviet times, was seen as a glamorous lifestyle by young girls throughout the Russian Federation.

Though feminism itself gained little ground in the popular consciousness during the 1990s, the culture of sex underwent a profound transformation. Before the late 1980s, virtually any discussion of sex in the media, in literature, or on screen was taboo. Now there were self-help books, talk shows, explicit films, and abundant pornography. In Russia, as elsewhere, feminists varied in their opinions about these new phenomena, most of which were dominated by a male perspective and orientation.

At the same time that America and Western Europe were beginning to wake up to the problems of sexual harassment and discrimination, Russia was moving in the opposite direction. Job announcements for secretaries looked more like personal ads, often specifying certain physical types, and sometimes including the barely coded phrase "no hang-ups" (*bez kompleksov*). When the Russian media reported on Western controversies over so-called "political correctness," the tone was usually amusement or disdain at the prudery of Westerns who have lost their knack at flirting and their ability to take a joke.[4]

Just as in the 1920s, the new sexual permissiveness sparked a backlash, but this time in the service of stricter governmental control and greater involvement of the Russian Orthodox Church. As the first decade of the twenty-first century drew to a close, more and more voices were raised calling for "morality" and a return to "traditional values." Such appeals had both internal and external roots. American right-wing evangelical groups saw the former Soviet Union as a land of opportunity. Though the increasingly strict laws regulating religion in 1997 and 2006 drastically decreased the influx of missionaries and proselytizers of all stripes, evangelical groups such as The World Congress of Families found allies in the Russian government, media, and civil society, supplying money and know-how to campaigns against abortion and homosexuality.[5]

By the time Pussy Riot staged its Punk Prayer, the forces of Russian conservatism and traditionalism had begun to focus their hostility on something called "gender ideology." This term has its roots in Vatican intellectual circles in the 1990s, and entered the public conversation in the West in 2003. Over the next decade, it spread throughout European countries with large Catholic populations, though Kevin Moss shows that it was used even earlier in Russian as a neutral term in the scholarly literature.[6] The term's Catholic origins may have delayed its adoption by conservatives in Russia, given the longstanding distrust of Catholicism within the Russian Orthodox Church.[7]

"Gender ideology" recasts feminist discussions of "gender" as a threat to human civilization. Where progressives view the idea of "gender" as liberatory (opening up the possibility for people to live and act in relative freedom from the roles ascribed to them by society's gendered assumptions), the crusaders against gender ideology argue that feminists are encouraging people to go against God and nature. The differences between men and women are biological (and even metaphysical), rather than the product of culture. Those who espouse gender ideology are encouraging men and women to abandon their natural functions (leadership and maternity, respectively). Positing homosexuality as natural, or saying that LGBT are "born this way," encourages children to step on the path of perversion.

On December 12, 2012, just two months after Pussy Riot's case was heard on appeal (when Katya was released), Putin made a speech in which he lamented that "today's Russian society is experiencing a clear lack of '*dukhovnye skrepy*'"[8] An odd phrase that immediately became a meme, "*dukhovnye skrepy*" literally means "spiritual braces," "spiritual supports," or even "spiritual staples" or "spiritual clamps." "Spiritual underpinnings" is probably better, though it does not capture the phrase's fundamental weirdness. But it was a harbinger of things to come: the proclamation of Russia's importance as the defender of "traditional values," the adoption of a law against so-called "homosexual propaganda" in 2013, the affirmation of marriage as the "union between a man and a woman" in 2015, and decriminalization of domestic battery in 2017. Thus Pussy Riot emerged within an environment of increasing social conservatism, and the backlash against the group may have even contributed to its codification.

Because of the scandal surrounding both their case and their performances, Pussy Riot has become the (masked) face of Russian feminism to much of the world. But accepting the equation of Pussy Riot and Russian feminism does a disservice to the many women in Russia who were involved in feminist activism long before anyone had ever heard of the punk actionist collective. While they never wielded significant power or influence, it was not for lack of trying.

Valerie Sperling interviewed seventeen feminist activists in 2012, after the women of Pussy Riot had been in jail for three months. She notes that all of her interview subjects supported Nadya, Masha, and Katya now that they were political prisoners, but some of them declined to recognize Pussy Riot as a "feminist endeavor." One was critical of the group's lyrics, which they saw as "embracing the idea of sexual objectification," concluding "it's not feminist discourse." Another lamented that Pussy Riot "expressed aggression through sex, that sex and violence were the same thing." Others called Pussy Riot's understanding of feminism "superficial" and "adolescent."[9]

There were famous feminists who did offer qualified support, notably Olga Lipovskaia. As Sperling writes:

> Lipovskaia argued in April 2012 that while Pussy Riot's songs "contained no ideological or conceptual feminist positions," their actions could certainly be considered feminist because they "truly break the traditional ideas about the female role. And in that sense, even without having a feminist message, they were still carrying out feminist action and making a feminist gesture."[10]

The internal Russian feminist controversies over Pussy Riot are not without precedent. Most progressive movements find themselves caught up in disputes over radicalism vs. proceduralism at some point or another. Before the Russian Revolution, the biggest schism in European feminist movements was over the question of priorities: should socialist feminists throw in their lot with revolutionary movements and expect their goals to be fulfilled as part of a broader program, or should they devote themselves exclusively to questions of sexual equality?[11] In the West, the so-called "liberal feminists" carried the day, working for change within the existing systems. In revolutionary Russia, as we have seen, feminism found itself assimilated in, if not coopted by, the Bolshevik agenda.

It should not be much of a surprise that Russia's best known feminist (or at least, the best known feminist before Pussy Riot), Maria Arbatova, had rather harsh words for the group. Arbatova is an author, journalist, television host, and politician; as the co-host of "I Myself" ("*Ia sama*"), the first weekly women's talk show in Russia, she brought new visibility to feminism (both as a word and a set of ideas). On the whole, Arbatova shared the opinion of many liberal commentators on the Pussy Riot affair, expressing disapproval of the group's activities but even harsher condemnation of their persecution by the state.

On March 7, 2013 (the eve of International Women's Day, which is widely celebrated in Russia), Arbatova appeared on a talk show hosted by Ksenia Sobchak (more on her in a bit) on the independent television station TV-Rain. The interview was as fascinating for its interpersonal dynamics as for its contents, because Sobchak and Arbatova clearly loathe each other.

In response to a question about Pussy Riot's role as feminist activists, Arbatova expressed horrified skepticism. Could Pussy Riot be the successors to Arbatova's generation of feminists? "God forbid!" She explains:

These people are engaged in post-modernism. They have absolutely not been spotted doing anything about the discrimination of women. They may have said something somewhere, like all civilized people. I feel very deeply for them in light of their punishment. But let's discuss the women's movement rather than those who use this word to describe qualitatively different things.[12]

Real feminists, according to Arbatova, do "real" work that helps women; it is much less flashy, but it is substantive. Sobchak keeps pressing Arbatova on the idea that the latter might simply be "out of date," but Arbatova refuses to engage with her on these terms. It would be easy to dismiss Arbatova here as old-fashioned or prudish, but this would be unfair. Arbatova is the same woman who told a reporter, "I have three erogenous zones: my children, men, and human rights".[13]

It is easy to make both too much and too little of the range of Russian feminist opinions on Pussy Riot. Expecting all feminists to move in lock-step and hold identical beliefs is not just unrealistic; it is the reduction of feminism to caricature.

Arbatova has a reasonable difference of opinion with Pussy Riot, but it makes sense that this disagreement would come out in an interview with Ksenia Sobchak. When it comes to Pussy Riot, Sobchak's approach always seemed to boil down to her trying to provoke a cat fight among feminists, and making sure that feminism cannot be taken seriously.

Ksenia Sobchak is one of the most famous people in the Russian Federation: the daughter of a man who was either the great democratic hope of St. Petersburg (according to mid-1990s Western media) or the cynical apparatchik who paved the way for Putin's rise to power (according to Masha Gessen, among others). Ksenia Sobchak became the face of rich Russian excess, the Putin-era Party Girl. As a reality show TV host and fixture of the gossip columns, Sobchak was an unlikely champion of the anti-Putin protest movement (or indeed, of anything political whatsoever). But her embrace of the opposition in 2011 appeared to signal a new seriousness of purpose. On TV-Rain, in her reinvention of herself as television journalist/host, Sobchak acquitted herself far better than her critics could have expected. She was smart and well-spoken, and usually managed to elicit interesting observations and replies from her guests.

But somehow, Pussy Riot was her kryptonite.

Not long after Katya was released from jail, Sobchak and fellow journalist Ksenia Sokolova interviewed her for a popular liberal web portal. The contrast between Katya and her interviewers (Sobchak and Sokolova) could not have been more pronounced.

Sobchak's questions verged on self-parody, beginning with this interchange about the founding of Pussy Riot:

**Sobchak:**   Was it at a party?

**Katya:**   We got together periodically, discussed some topics and events in Russia. Sexism, of course.

**Sobchak:**   I'm trying to understand how young, pretty girls could get together and talk about sexism! For example, I can't imagine me and Sokolova getting together and talking about sexism, and not, say, guys. Of course, we could come up with a plan to do something nasty, like, for example, decide that all our former boyfriends who are parliament members are assholes and we'll use some well-chosen words to f*ck them up.

**Katya:** You'd be surprised, but there are feminist girls who discuss sexism. They encounter sexism every day. Unfortunately, our society is permeated with sexism.[14]

Same planet, different worlds. Sobchak did follow up with some incisive questions about whether or not Katya's suspended sentence lent legitimacy to an otherwise absurd trial, and about the irony of an anonymous feminist group whose most recognizable member (Nadya) looks like a "cover girl."

But Sobchak followed her interview with a blog post entitled "Who is Yekaterina Samutsevich?"[15] She starts with the assertion that Pussy Riot was about young girls wanting attention, with the feminist rationale added later. Then she dismisses Katya's politics as a cover for personal woes: "Katya is clearly struggling with something inside herself. I don't know what. Maybe she wasn't loved enough, maybe there was a trauma, maybe it's a rejection of herself in the body in which she exists—I don't know. But I have the feeling that her actions look more like a struggle not for feminism, but with her own fears, complexes, and internal problems." She ends with a fantasy of Katya setting this life aside and marrying an IT oligarch. This was either very strange irony, thinly veiled queerbaiting, or profound cluelessness.

Sobchak managed to score the first interview with Masha and Nadya upon their release from their respective prison camps, flying out to meet them in the North before their return to Moscow.[16] Her first question to the most famous anti-capitalist activists in Russia was about money and profit ("How much is the Pussy Riot brand worth?"). Masha and Nadya try to explain their complete lack of interest in this question, but Sobchak simply will not let it go, moving on to concerts and European tours.

From there, she tries to turn the Pussy Riot story into a tale of gossip and conflict ("Masha, are you mad that Nadya gets so much attention?" Is it "fair" that Masha had to fly so far to see Nadya?), eventually comparing them to the Beatles and Destiny's Child. The interview ends at its lowest point, when Sobchak inquires about Masha's beauty regime ("I can't not ask the most important question—what's up with your eyebrows?").[17]

There is something deeply entertaining about this spectacle; Masha's and Nadya's unflappability completely undermines Sobchak's familiar TV persona. By the end, Sobchak, who had started out addressing both women informally ("ty") gets so flustered that she finds herself switching to the formal "vy".

Certainly, Sobchak has troubles understanding their version of feminism. But the problem is much greater than that. Sobchak is flatfooted by Pussy Riot's complete rejection of the entire culture that spawned her: the world of money, power, and glamour. Whatever their political views, nearly all of Sobchak's previous interview subjects had one thing in common: they were all celebrities. Sobchak, like much of the Russian media, seems incapable of believing that there are people in Russia who are indifferent to fame and fortune. A common dismissal of Pussy Riot (once made by Putin himself) is that they were just trying to get publicity for themselves.[18] But, as Masha and Nadya themselves pointed out at their press conference upon their arrival in Moscow, Pussy Riot is anonymous by definition, and their identities were revealed against their will.

Sobchak's failure to connect with Pussy Riot says a lot about her, but its significance is much broader. With her questions about money, rivalry, and make-up, Sobchak demonstrates the problem that has rendered Pussy Riot all but illegible to the Russian media. The political culture of the past two decades has fostered a corrosive cynicism that is so widespread as to be taken for granted. There is little room in the public political discourse for seriously entertaining the idea that one could be so motivated by political and artistic ideals as to put personal concerns on the back burner (without joining a convent or a monastery).

By virtue of their scandalous performances and outrageous trial, Pussy Riot brought feminism back into the Russian public eye. But the nature of this publicity and its results are not what Westerners might expect. The Western media were head over heels about Pussy Riot; the familiar frame of an oppressive Russian government cracking down on heroic fighters for freedom was easily adapted to the Pussy Riot story. Their feminism was easily assimilated into the same framework, especially since women's political movements are generally portrayed in a more positive light in Europe and the United States.

In Russia, their feminism was both more of a problem and more problematic. Feminist activists offered reasoned, justifiable criticism of Pussy Riot's approach, a fact that also would not be a great surprise in the West. Decades of exposure to feminism in mainstream Western cultures means that audiences were more likely to be familiar with the idea that feminists can disagree with each other on substantive issues. (This is one of the reasons why many prefer to speak of "feminisms" rather than feminism.)

On Russian television, however, Pussy Riot runs the risk of representing *all* feminism, a problem that only grows more acute if one considers just how Pussy Riot gets represented. We saw the demonization of Pussy Riot (and, by extension, feminism) in the *Provocateurs* documentaries, but even more liberal outlets such as TV-Rain and the web portal Snob gave airtime and bandwidth to Sobchak's trivialization of the entire Pussy Riot project. Ironically, Sobchak reduces Pussy Riot through a process of feminization, insisting that the very fact of their womanhood means that they must be understood through mainstream clichés and stereotypes.

Sobchak put Nadya and Masha in a precarious position; if they objected too strongly to her focus on the girly side of things, they could conform to Russian stereotypes of feminists as puritanical "bluestockings" (a term that is current in Russian as opposed to historical in English). As we shall see in the next chapter, they (particularly Nadya) pursued a much more complicated strategy, leaving a space for glamour and beauty without letting themselves be defined by it.

# CHAPTER 10
# ANONYMITY AND GLAMOUR: WHO
# WAS THAT MASKED WOMAN?

Masha, Katya, and Nadya have the most famous Russian faces ever to be concealed behind masks. Theirs is an odd kind of notoriety: in their home country, they are best known for publicly hiding their identities.

The impact of the masked face in post-Soviet Russia is not immediately evident to outsiders, particularly to Americans. Though there were masquerades and costume parties before the 1917 Revolution, the Soviet Union had no tradition comparable to Halloween or *Dia de los Muertos*. Soviet mass culture had no room for masked adventurers or caped crusaders. What traditions of anonymity do exist are hardly laudable, and this brings us back to dissent: in the Brezhnev era, dissent meant signing your name to an open letter, or publicly expressing an inexpressible view. In the few cases where identities were hidden behind pseudonyms, the sheer evil of the culprits seemed magnified in the state media (see the repeated characterization of the underground writers Sinyavsky and Daniel, who published abroad under other names, as "turncoats" and "changelings").[1] Anonymity was largely the preserve of the informers, the authors of anonymous denunciations that led to prison sentences for those denounced.

The situation has changed since 1991, but only somewhat. Halloween has made some small inroads, but religious leaders routinely denounce it as satanic.[2] Covering one's face in public is still illegal (as it is in many other parts of the world), with one major exception: the special forces known as OMON (the Russian equivalent to SWAT) routinely wear ski masks when making arrests or storming buildings.

However, Pussy Riot's use of nicknames has deep Russian roots. Schoolchildren in particular are likely to call friends by nicknames (whether or not this is because of the relative lack of variety in first names given to Russian children is a matter of speculation). Gangsters and criminals almost always have a nickname, at least in film and fiction, while the proliferation of playful handles on the internet is a phenomenon that knows no borders. Where Pussy Riot is unique in Russia is in the combination of masks and nicknames in an attempt to ensure true anonymity.

The most obvious precedent for this combination is the American tradition of superheroes. Though not all of them wear masks, very few go by their real names: Batman, Spider-Man, and Ms. Marvel all cover their faces and hide their secret identities. Indeed, Katya, Nadya, and Masha refer to Pussy Riot as superheroes on multiple occasions.[3] While this is a comparison that most Russians could now be expected to understand (thanks to the twenty-first century superhero conquest of the multiplex), there is little about this context that is actually Russian. Comic books were condemned as trash entertainment in Soviet times; they only started to make inroads in the late 1980s.[4] While many American superhero comics now exist in Russian translation, the comics created by Russians rarely make use of the superhero genre.[5]

Virtually everything about the superhero was antithetical to Soviet culture: the tendency to work outside the system rather than as part of recognized law enforcement (vigilantism); the emphasis on individual character and motivation rather than collectivism; and, of course, the concealment of the hero's identity. Though there is a strong tradition of interpreting the superhero as the champion of the status quo (and therefore a lapdog to those in power), both the development of the modern (post-1960s) superhero and the circumstances of actual authoritarian rule tend to place the masked vigilante in an oppositional role.[6] Look no further than the adoption of the Guy Fawkes mask— worn by the anarchist protagonist of both the graphic novel *V for Vendetta* and its film adaption—by the Anonymous hacker collective.

In the hands of Anonymous, that Guy Fawkes mask has a very different function from the traditional superhero mask. In the comic, it belongs to one person, only to be taken up by another once her predecessor has died; the lesson she learns is to submerge both her own identity and any curiosity she had about the previous V beneath an image that represents that cause. Anonymous seems to be building on the movie, which ends with a crowd of people all covering their faces with identical Guy Fawkes masks, creating a collective anonymity predicated on their common indistinguishable features.

The balaclavas worn by Pussy Riot operate in a space somewhere between the superhero and *V for Vendetta*/Anonymous. The masks conceal the women's identity (the traditional concern of the superhero) while also denying the prerogative of the male gaze to see and evaluate a woman's face. But the balaclavas do not function exactly like Guy Fawkes masks. For one, they allow the face to remain expressive, unlike the rigid, kabuki-like masks of Anonymous. For another, they occlude individuality without excising it: the balaclavas resemble each other without being identical, and, as a result, that same formulation describes the women who wear them. Anonymity does not have to be the same as identity.

But the balaclava resembles the Guy Fawkes mask in another way: it is a productive pattern for a mask rather than a specific mask for a specific person. Anyone can put on a balaclava and be Pussy Riot (as the women of Pussy Riot say repeatedly), but putting on a Batman mask does not make someone Batman.[7] In Pussy Riot's hands, the balaclava, which takes its name from a battle in the Crimean War, moves from the world of male military violence to female domestic handicrafts: not only can anyone put on a balaclava, virtually anyone can make one.

The gender politics of Pussy Riot's balaclava become clear when we once again compare them to the other feminist group with which Pussy Riot has so often been linked in the post-Soviet public consciousness: Femen. Femen's radical response to the objectification of women is to dispense with mystery and allure by baring their breasts in public, implicitly demanding that their half-naked bodies not be treated as mere sex objects. Pussy Riot stands out for covering up what was is usually public (the face), turning the face into an object of art rather than objects of desire.

The bright color palette of both the balaclavas and their outfits are not fashion statements, but anti-fashion statements, demanding that the women be looked at as compositions of color in motion. Many have noted the visual similarity between Pussy Riot's balaclavas and the paintings of the Russian avant-garde artist Kazimir Malevich, whose portrayal of both men and women reduced them to geometric figures and color with virtually no features.[8] This is a kind of anonymity that stands out rather than withdraws, and can be recognized from a mile away.

The secret identities of Pussy Riot are a significant step in the women's evolution from their origins in Voina. Voina, despite its anarchist politics, was personality driven (witness the split between the Moscow and St. Petersburg branches). Though nearly everyone in Voina had a nickname (Petya the Piggy, Tolokno), these were performative affectations rather than a means of concealment. Both Nadya and Petya were fairly well-known before the Punk Prayer, thanks to their Voina activities. Certainly, their performance in the Zoological Museum was unforgettable. If the Russian media-consuming public had been asked to vote someone "most likely to be a secret member of Pussy Riot," Nadya would have won first place.

This is not the only prize Nadya could have won. Skipping ahead a bit to her time in prison, one of the many news stories about Nadya's conflicts with the camp authorities took a surreal turn. On July 26, 2013, Nadya was denied parole due to numerous violations of camp rules, including her refusal to take part in a "Miss Charm" prison camp beauty contest. In a speech before the court, Nadya used the "Miss Charm" event as an example of the absurdity of the Putin regime:

> And so, if you are a woman, and what is more if you are a young woman and even the slightest bit attractive, then you are basically required to take part in beauty contests. If you refuse to participate, you will be denied parole, based on your disdain for the "Miss Charm" event. In the opinion of the prison colony administration and the court that supports it, non-participation means that you lack a "positive attitude." However, I claim that in boycotting the beauty contest I express my own principled and painstakingly formulated "positive attitude." My own position, in distinction from the conservative, secret-police aesthetic of

the camp administration, consists in reading my books and journals during moments that I extract by force from the deadening daily schedule of the prison colony.[9]

Could there be a more perfect encapsulation of Nadya's double-bind after she was outed as a member of Pussy Riot? The face hidden behind the balaclava was, by all conventional standards, beautiful. Quite simply, the camera loved Nadya Tolokonnikova, even when Nadya Tolokonnikova had no interest in trading on her looks. Singling out Nadya is awkward, since it threatens to view her, Masha, and Katya as engaged in a "Miss Charm" competition of their own, perhaps the most reflexively sexist way of dismissing the serious aspirations of young women. This was one of Ksenia Sobchak's tactics in her egregious interview of Masha and Nadya right after their release. Sobchak's ridiculous comparisons of Pussy Riot to the Beatles and Destiny Child pointed to one disturbing aspect of the circulation of the PR defendants' images: as if they were just members of a "girl band," Nadya becomes "the pretty one," Katya "the tough one," and Masha ... the smart one".[10] Sobchak tries to provoke Nadya and Masha into a (pussy)cat fight by drawing attention to Nadya's beauty, attempting to goad Masha into expressing some form of jealousy. Her insinuations are insulting on a number of levels, but the two former prisoners refuse to be provoked.

Perhaps a better way of describing Nadya's image is that she has *glamour*. Glamour is a term that took off in Russian in the early 2000s, usually in reference to the lifestyles of the rich and famous.[11] In Nadya's case, glamour could be a tool for her to exploit or a trap to avoid. In a discussion during Nadya's visit to New York University in 2016, she briefly addressed the question, saying that she saw no contradiction between feminist idealism and personal style. This is a particularly valuable approach to take in Russia, overtly dismissing the longstanding stereotype of feminists as "bluestockings."

But the possible exploitation of Nadya's image is a problem not just because of gender and feminism. Anonymity shielded Pussy Riot from all the accusations usually employed to undermine people seen as ideological crusaders, especially in the cynical atmosphere of post-Soviet

Russia: the charge that the people in question are only interested in "PR" (a foreign abbreviation that has become its own verb in Russian, "*piarit'sia*"), and the charge that they're in it for the money. True, the purveyors of conspiracy on Channel One repeatedly claimed that Pussy Riot must be financed by sinister, possibly foreign, powers, but they could say that about anyone.[12] In Pussy Riot's case, nothing they were doing provided an obvious means for generating filthy lucre.

It did not take long for Masha and particularly Nadya to prove vulnerable to accusations that they were "selling out." Within a few weeks of the women's release, Russian social media went Code Red over Nadya's appearance in, of all things, a fashion shoot. To make matters worse, the shoot was for a company whose name sounds as though it were slapped together by a Random Capitalist Epithet Generator: "TrendsBrands."

Only a few months before, Nadya had taken a principled stand in refusing to participate in a beauty contest, and now she was modeling clothes. On a human level, it's worth recalling that Nadya had just spent nearly two years in a prison colony. If she wanted to dress up now that she was out, that was her business. Except that she was an anti-capitalist crusader who had repeatedly expressed nothing but disdain for . . . trends and brands.

Nadya quickly engaged in damage control on her Facebook page, explaining that TrendsBrands helped her when she was imprisoned, sending her clothes, which she wore and passed on to other inmates. She also insisted that she received no money for the session. In an interview, she called this an "important story about socially responsible business, which needs to be developed and supported." This is a perfectly understandable, classically liberal approach to the intersection of commerce and social engagement. But it is not what was expected of Nadya Tolokonnikova.

On Facebook, she brushed off concerns about being coopted in a back-and-forth in the comments on her initial TrendsBrands post. Some commenters expressed sympathy, while others gave a harsh assessment of her actions (and one simply posted a facepalm gif). Nadya's response: "I'm playing with capitalism, and capitalism is playing with me." To which someone immediately replied: "Nadya,

IMHO, it's hard to play with capitalism. It always wins. You can walk away with it, but you can never beat it."

This incident, largely forgotten over the course of the news cycle, should be seen in the larger context of supporters' concern about Pussy Riot's circulation within a capitalist ecosystem. Hence the numerous press reports while the women were still in jail about the question of the "Pussy Riot brand." "Experts" were consulted to assess just how much this as yet non-existent brand might be worth (answer: a lot), even as the women themselves denied any interest in such an activity. Eventually, they changed their mind, deciding to pursue the possibility, but only to prevent others from doing so. The press reported that Petya was trying to register the brand and pass himself off as the Pussy Riot spokesman, which was the likely cause for a letter the women wrote in prison condemning him for "betrayal" (they all seem to have made up since then). After firing her lawyers, Katya claimed that one of them, Mark Feigin, had been trying to register the brand through his wife's company. Feigin countered by charging that it was Katya who was trying to commercialize Pussy Riot for her own gain.[13]

On June 13, 2015, a YouTube account devoted primarily to videos by the anonymous members of Pussy Riot posted a brief clip entitled "Pyotr Verzilov's Conversation with Mark Feign in May 2012," which is purported to be a deleted scene from the 2013 documentary *Pussy Riot: A Punk Prayer*.[14] Most of the four-and-a-half minute video consists of the two men sitting in a restaurant, with Feigin doing most of the talking and Petya doing most of the eating. For the first half, Feign is discussing the legal case (which makes sense, since he is the defendants' lawyer). Then Feigin turns to marketing and branding, repeatedly mentioning the idea of having Julia Ormond star in a film about the Pussy Riot case. Feigin pushes for signing a contract and arranging terms, while Petya says, "Let's not get ahead of ourselves." But he also says, "I agree with you." Feigin pushes further, insisting that Petya bring these issues up with Nadya, since he's afraid of her reaction ("She'll eat me alive"). It's an unpleasant scene: the women are in prison while the men are talking about making a deal.

At their joint press conference following their release from prison, Nadya addressed the brand question directly:

We discussed this possibility in the summer of 2012—putting money into support for the development of civil society, of feminist and charitable organizations.... But we realized that this is not our story, and we can't manage the brand: if we get tied up in the brand, it's too easy to accuse us of misappropriating resources, because it will be very hard to demonstrate and maintain transparency of the financial flows.[15]

Of course, all of this begs the question: what standing do Masha, Nadya, and Katya have to claim the brand as their own? There were (and are) other members of Pussy Riot—an organization that was avowedly leaderless. The likelihood of any meaningful contact, let alone consultation, between the imprisoned women and their anonymous comrades was slim to none.

At various moments after their release, when Masha and Nadya would speak at public events, they would say again and again that, when they appeared without masks, they were not Pussy Riot, since Pussy Riot cannot be reconciled with public identity. But this distinction was usually lost on the people inviting them or discussing them, who would refer to them as "Pussy Riot" in promotional materials.

On February 6, 2014, six women signing themselves as "anonymous members of Pussy Riot" using their pseudonyms (Garadja, Fara, Shaiba, Cat, Seraphima and Schumacher) issued a public letter about this very concern. First, they thanked all their supporters, and expressed their joy at the recent release of Nadya and Masha. But they also had harsh words for the women whose names were permanently associated with their movement, which are worth quoting at length:

*We are very pleased with Masha's and Nadya's release.*
*[. . .]*
*Unfortunately for us, they are being so carried away with the problems in Russian prisons, that they completely forgot about the aspirations and ideals of our group—feminism, separatist resistance, fight against authoritarianism and personality cult, all of which, as a matter of fact, were the cause for their unjust punishment.*

*Now it is no secret that Masha and Nadya are no longer members of the group, and they will no longer take part in radical activism. Now they are engaged in a new project. Now they are institutionalized advocates of prisoners' rights.*

*And as you know, such advocacy is hardly compatible with radical political statements and provocative works of art that raise controversial topics in modern society. Just as gender-conformity is not compatible with radical feminism.*

*Institutionalized advocacy can hardly afford the critique of fundamental norms and rules that underline the very mechanics of modern patriarchal society. Being an institutional part of this society, such advocacy, can hardly go beyond the rules set forth by this society.*

*Yes, we lost two friends, two ideological fellow member[s], but the world has acquired two brave, interesting, controversial human rights defenders—fighters for the rights of the Russian prisoners.*

*Unfortunately, we cannot congratulate them on this in person, because they refuse to have any contact with us. But we appreciate their choice and sincerely wish them well in their new career.*

*At the moment, we are witnessing an outrageous collision.*

*While Nadya and Masha are being the focus of media and the international community, they gather crowds of journalists and people heed to their every word, so far no one hears them.*

*In almost every interview they repeat [that] they left the group, that they are no longer Pussy Riot, that they act in their own names, that they will no longer engage in radical art activities. However, the headlines are still full of the group's name, all their public appearances are declared as performances of Pussy Riot, and their personal withdrawal from Pussy Riot is treated as termination of the entire collective, thus ignoring the fact that at the pulpit of the Christ the Savior Church, there were not two, but five women in balaclavas and the Red Square performance had eight participants.*

*The apotheosis of this misunderstanding was the public announcement by Amnesty International of Masha's and Nadya's speech at a concert in the Barclays Center in New York, as the first legal performance of Pussy Riot.*

*Moreover, instead of the names of Nadya and Masha, the poster of the event showed a man in a balaclava with electric guitar, under the name of Pussy Riot, while the organizers called for people to buy expensive tickets.*

*All this is an extreme contradiction to the very principles of Pussy Riot collective.*

*We are all-female separatist collective—no man can represent us either on a poster or in reality.*

*We belong to leftist anti-capitalist ideology–we charge no fees for viewing our art-work, all our videos are distributed freely on the web, the spectators to our performances are always spontaneous passers by, and we never sell tickets to our "shows."*

*Our performances are always "illegal," staged only in unpredictable locations and public places not designed for traditional entertainment. The distribution of our clips is always through free and unrestricted media channels.*

*We are anonymous, because we act against any personality cult, against hierarchies implied by appearance, age and other visible social attributes. We cover our heads, because we oppose the very idea of using female face as a trademark for promoting any sort of goods or services.*

*The mixing of the rebel feminist punk image with the image of institutionalized defenders of prisoners' rights, is harmful for us as a collective, as well as it is harmful for the new role that Nadya and Masha have taken on.*

*Hear them finally!*

*Since it happened that Nadya and Masha chose not to be with us, please, respect their choice. Remember, we are no longer Nadya and Masha. They are no longer Pussy Riot.*

*The campaign "Free Pussy Riot" is over. We, as art collective, have an ethical right to preserve our art practice, our name and our visual identity, distinct from other organizations.*[16]

Though the letter hints at some degree of conflict between the anonymous signatories and the no-longer anonymous Masha and Nadya, to focus on these possible tensions would be to continue on in the Sobchak mode of Pussy Riot coverage: trying to turn an ideological movement into the stuff of celebrity scandal. I have no hard information about this conflict, and little inclination to seek it out.

Instead, the letter skillfully exposes the basic problem of the then-current presentation of Nadya and Masha. A brand-obsessed media needs the words "Pussy Riot" to draw attention; more charitably, "Pussy Riot" has greater name recognition and is easier for non-Russians to pronounce than "Tolokonnikova" or "Alyokhina." Ironically, this is a complete reversal from Pussy Riot's initial situation in Russia, where the group's name was foreign, difficult to pronounce, and not always easy to comprehend, while the last names of the women arrested were simple and intelligible.

The letter also demands that the world acknowledge that Nadya and Masha, in their new public roles (which will be discussed in more detail in the next chapter) are not only not speaking in Pussy Riot's name, but are engaged in activities that, however praiseworthy, have nothing to do with the aesthetics, tactics, and goals of the anonymous punk collective.

Moreover, even if we momentarily accept the identification of these two women with Pussy Riot, the Barclays Center publicity betrays a fundamental misunderstanding of what Pussy Riot was about. Certainly, choosing to portray a man in a balaclava is baffling, but even the electric guitar is misleading: this is an instrument that Nadya and Masha could barely play. Granted, limited musical talent was rarely an obstacle for punk bands, but equating Pussy Riot with a punk band is reductive. The Western entertainment industry wants and needs them to be a punk band: this makes them sexy, and it also flatters the egos of Western performers whose occasional forays into politics would put them in the same category as a group of women who used music to make a larger point, rather than musicians whose use their celebrity as a personal or political platform.

For Masha and Nadya, losing anonymity was clearly a blessing and a curse.

Pussy Riot complicated efforts to assess the "enemy's" strength, in that it was fighting an anonymous, guerrilla grrl war. Conducting a series of public actions and internet appearances without revealing the participants' identity may well be a bigger scandal than the group's foul-mouthed feminism. Judging from the media coverage (and, of course, the state prosecution), the existence of an anonymous collective that gives little evidence of self-interest is an almost unassimilable data point.

In his famous response to the Roland Barthes essay "Death of the Author," the French philosopher Michel Foucault proposes an archeology of authorship, noting that the author as a function only becomes important as an object of payment or punishment: who gets the credit, and who gets the blame?[17] The Russian legal system was clearly preoccupied with the latter point, but the media focused more on the former. Every time that the members of Pussy Riot were asked about money and profits, they expressed their categorical disinterest in the group's commercial potential. Yet rumors had it that the group is planning a European tour of stadium-sized venues, and the Russian media could not get enough of the question of Pussy Riot's registration as a brand.[18] Both the unmasked members of the group and their former lawyers framed the question of the brand in terms of protecting it from exploitation, rather than exploiting it themselves. But talk of profit and commercialization continued.

Of course, this is the nature of the modern capitalist media: selling and merchandizing are fundamental to the system, and one could argue that it is all but impossible for the media to conceive of disinterested cultural production. Yet a quick comparative glance at capitalist mediascapes in a variety of countries reveals that there are plenty of ways in which the media can frame an activity as non-commercial: in the US, for instance, one frequently finds the presentation of people whose activities are interpreted as charitable or simply ideological. This does not mean that there isn't a commercial component, or that, as Slavoj Zizek argues, the very notion of philanthropy simply props up an unjust system.[19] But the Russian media were constantly trying to follow a money trail for which they could find no evidence.

The political ramifications are, of course, clear. What better way to attack an anti-capitalist movement than by showing money as the primary motivation? And what better affirmation of the idea that modern Russia is a place where only self-interest is conceivable? But there is much more at work here. First, there is garden variety sexism:

for many of the collective's critics, the idea that a group of "girls" could do something like this on their own simply did not compute. Clearly, there has to be a man behind it all. The most common candidate is Petya; as the head of Voina, he's a familiar "enemy" figure, and as Masha's husband, he is, by patriarchal definition, the boss.[20] Beyond him, the media quickly named the usual suspects (mostly disgraced oligarchs).

Here we are also dealing with rather straightforward and widespread conspiratorial thought more than simply sexism: Russia is once again a victim of a plot by foreign enemies.[21] Protodiakon (Protodeacon) Andrei Kuraev sees Pussy Riot as part of a liberal attack on Russia and the Orthodox Church:

> I'm afraid that behind [Pussy Riot] is a serious group of people with harsh ideas about what the world should be … These are the forces of liberalism, but they behave in an extremely totalitarian fashion … This is not the action of some strange girls acting alone [*strannyx odinochek*]; behind them is a very serious ideological system that permits itself everything, but permits Christians nothing.[22]

Latter-day Eurasianist Aleksandr Dugin sees these "porno-hooligans" as "scapegoats" and a "fifth column" in an "information war" conducted by then-American Ambassador Michael McFaul against Russian statehood and the Russian Orthodox Church.[23]

Unmasked, Pussy Riot is vulnerable to the powerful machinery of celebrity and glamor, even if their involvement is entirely against their will. Here we have the ultimate irony of Pussy Riot: a group that spreads its message through anonymous viral video is undermined by mainstream video technology's fascination with a pretty face. Video killed the anonymous star.

# CHAPTER 11
# QUIET RIOT?

When Nadya and Masha were granted early release by President Putin (presumably to avoid bad PR during the upcoming Winter Olympics in Sochi), they would have encountered the usual problems faced by former prisoners upon their return to society: reintegrating with their family, adjusting to relative freedom after two years of confinement. The unusual question before them was: would they now become prisoners of their own celebrity? What exactly do two formerly anonymous punk actionists anarchists do next?

Had they consulted with Katya, they would have quickly seen how differently their futures were developing. Katya, who had the good fortune to be released before her comrades were sent away, did the expected interview circuit. But her conviction was not overturned; living under a suspended sentence, she would have had good reason to fear getting involved in public political activity. Of course, she still had her credentials as a computer programmer, but after the Pussy Riot affair, she was effectively unemployable. In 2017, one news article quoted an anonymous "friend" claiming that Katya was working as a waitress, but just six months earlier she explained in an extended interview that she was studying computational linguistics.[1]

By contrast, Masha and Nadya had served real time, and continued to be a cause célèbre long after Katya faded from public view. Though much of the speculation about their future income was aimed at discrediting them, it was unlikely that Nadya and Masha would be leaving the public eye any time soon.

And indeed, when they held a marathon press conference in Moscow after their release, they presented a thorough and well-developed plan of action, one that leveraged their newfound fame for a larger purpose. That purpose had little to do with art or performance, and instead was more in keeping with what one might expect from dissidents.

Their overall focus was now about civil society, but the first project they unveiled was a direct result of their prison experience. After relating several harrowing tales, not about themselves, but about "ordinary" inmates, they announced their intent to found an organization dedicated to the rights of the imprisoned.[2] Called "Zona prava" ("Zone of Law"), it was a play on words. In Russian, the entire prison camp system is usually referred to simply as "the zone," so the "zone" of the organization's name had a double meaning.

Though "Zona prava" was clearly well planned, and continues to be active to this day, the very fact that Nadya and Masha intended to devote a significant amount of their time and energy to prisoners' rights is consistent with the improvisational impulse that has characterized their political and artistic development since before either of them joined Pussy Riot. Just as Pussy Riot eschewed foolish consistency, Masha and Nadya were determined to fight for justice where and how they deemed necessary, based on the problems they encountered. If anyone was wondering how prison might change them, the answer was simple: it turned their attention towards prison.

Once again, the two women showed how inadequate the "music group" framework was to Pussy Riot. In the West, plenty of famous pop stars are involved in political and charity work, but how many of them all but abandon performance to do so?

Nonetheless, after they spent a considerable amount of time during their press conference talking about prison issues, they were still met with misaddressed questions about concerts and world tours. A journalist from the tabloid *Moskovskii komsomolets*, acknowledging their declaration that they were no longer Pussy Riot, asked if they had come up with a "new name for their duo or trio." Their answer: "Our human rights organization has a name: 'Zona Prava.'"[3]

Zona Prava's website (zonaprava.com) is as practical as Pussy Riot's videos are provocative. The landing page, consisting of four different black-and-white photos taken in various parts of the prison system (and featuring primarily men), draws the eye to simple, forceful statement: "'Zona Prava' brings together people who want to achieve positive change in the sphere of human rights in Russia." There is even a page where people can write in with very specific questions and receive answers from a lawyer. The banner on the top of each page provides a phone number for inquiries.

Less than a year later, in September of 2014, Masha and Nadya founded an internet news outlet, MediaZona, a wide-ranging portal that pays special attention to questions of civil and human rights, and, of course, the legal system. MediaZona's founding was timely, as more and more Russian news outlets were encountering censorship and pressure from the state. Given MediaZona's profile and its notoriety (Petya is the publisher), the fact that it is still licensed in the Russian Federation is surprising.

In an interview with Reuters, Nadya declared: "The real punk is to build institutions."[4] It's an attention-getting statement, but dubious on the face of it. If anyone else had made this statement, it would have had all the punch of a public service announcement proclaiming that "real rebels look both ways when crossing the street." Not to mention how similar it is to the Russian feminist critiques of Pussy Riot described in Chapter 9.

Surely Nadya is savvier than that, so it is worth attempting to see what she might mean. In a country where legal and state institutions are increasingly vulnerable to the whims of those in power, the standard punk anti-institutional posture might be not only counter-productive, but, perversely, conservative or conformist. In this context, punk as a revolutionary force might choose institution-building as a radical strategy. Aesthetically speaking, though, there's nothing punk about editorial board meetings and conferring with counsel. It's a far cry from "Kill the Sexist."

Whether or not we accept that the important institution-building work initiated by Masha and Nadya was somehow radical and punk, it is just as hard to apply these qualifiers to their post-incarceration video performances. Now openly posting under the name Pussy Riot, Nadya (sometimes with Masha, sometimes without) released several musical clips on the internet, and the contrast with the early Pussy Riot recordings could not be more stark. Where Pussy Riot's videos were carefully edited archives of live happenings, these videos were just that: music videos.

They were, however, still explicitly political. In February of 2016, Nadya starred (!) in a video called "Chaika," a reference to opposition leader Alexei Navalny's exposé of Russian Prosecutor General Yuri Chaika's alleged corruption. Nadya and a group of young women, all dressed in Russian police uniforms, dance in offices, torture chambers, and prison cells while Nadya raps in the first person, speaking for Chaika himself. Her rap is a rhymed litany of Chaika's offenses, punctuated by scenes of Nadya looking at the camera while waving her hands in the form of a bird's wings (in addition to being the prosecutor's surname, "chaika" is Russian for "seagull"). The video makes its points boldly and clearly, but with none of the punk anarchism of the early Pussy Riot performances.

Though the video was accompanied by English subtitles, the target audience was internal to the Russian Federation (if nothing else, outsiders would have required extensive annotations to get the references). One year earlier, in February 2015, Nadya and Masha produced a video whose audience was meant to be far wider: "I Can't Breathe." For one thing, the lyrics were sung in English. For another, the immediate context was specifically American. "I can't breathe" were the last words spoken by Eric Garner before he died during his arrest by NYPD officers in Staten Island. Garner's argument with the police, culminating in his shouts of "I can't breathe" when they have him in a chokehold, replace the vocals for the last minute of the video.

"I Can't Breathe" is a rare kind of Pussy Riot performance, if it even can be called that, given the problems with Nadya and Masha appearing unmasked under that name. Where Pussy Riot's punk performances had been raw, rarely pretty, but always politically sophisticated, "I Can't Breathe" is aesthetically beautiful, but politically naive.

Even more than "Chaika," "I Can't Breathe" is a completely different sound for Pussy Riot. The instruments were played by Andrew Wyatt, Nick Zinner, vocals provided by Jack Wood, and the music composed by Scofferlane. The sound is smooth and professional. As for Nadya and Masha? A cynic would say that their job was, quite simply, to lie there.

Masha and Nadya explained that the change in musical style was deliberate:

The genre of this isn't like other Pussy Riot songs. It's an industrial ballad. Dark and urban. The rhythm and beat of the song is a metaphor of a heartbeat, the beat of a heart before it's about to stop. The absence of our usual aggressive punk vocals in this song is a reaction to this tragedy.[5]

Most of the video consists of Masha and Nadya, dressed in the uniforms of OMON (the Russian SWAT team), lying in a shallow grave while dirt is shoveled on to them. The scene is made even more eerie by the accelerated speed of the video track (burying them alive would presumably have taken more than four minutes), rendering their occasional movements and facial expressions oddly jerky. One of the few continuities with past Pussy Riot performances (not to mention Masha's subsequent work) is the willingness to put their own bodies in situations that look precarious and unpleasant. The expressions on their faces as the dirt hits them look unrehearsed; their eyes are closed, so they never know where the dirt is going to land. As the grave fills in, it covers their faces in a particularly disturbing manner, obscuring Masha's eyes but leaving much of her face initially untouched, while covering one side of Nadya's face more than the other. Eventually, their bodies and faces disappear from view.

This is an exquisitely produced video. What, then, could be the problem? The text accompanying the clip gives a hint: "This song is for Eric and for all those from Russia to America and around the globe who suffer from state terror—killed, choked, perished because of war and state sponsored violence of all kinds." In the best traditions of progressive coalition building, Nadya and Masha refuse to view a single instance of lethal police brutality as an isolated incident. For them, particularly as anarchists, all cases of "state terror" are essentially the same, since it is the power of the state apparatus that allows them (or perhaps even requires them) to happen.

This, then, explains their OMON uniforms, and the appearance of a pack of cigarettes with Russian, rather than English, writing in the first frame. The pack is a visual reminder that Garner was stopped by the police for selling loose cigarettes, an infraction for which he had been cited previously. But the Russian words, in addition to including the mandated warning that "smoking kills" (doubly ironic in Garner's case), indicate that the brand is "Russian Spring," a reference to the Russian Federation's "patriotic" involvement in Crimea and Eastern Ukraine.

As Luke Harding explains in *The Guardian*:

> I Can't Breathe is also a powerful protest against the political situation in Russia, and President Vladimir Putin's bloody undercover war in Ukraine. The video echoes the secret night-time burials of hundreds of Russian soldiers who have perished in the conflict. Their families are not told how their loved ones have died or where, Pussy Riot said, adding that such information "is forbidden". The Kremlin officially denies that its army is fighting in eastern Ukraine.[6]

The connection between the war in Ukraine and the Eric Garner case is, of course, tenuous. It is also a minefield, but one that Nadya and Masha apparently failed to recognize. While their writings and interviews have demonstrated a great deal of sympathy to the plight of racial minorities throughout the world, they seem to have missed the racial implications of their use (some would say "appropriation") of Garner's story. Tolerance for white artists using black stories and black bodies for political statements in their work, even for supportive political statements, has plummeted in recent years. For two white women to commemorate Garner's death by making a video in which their white bodies are the object of violence is, at least in the American context, problematic. Not being American, Masha and Nadya are probably not even used to thinking of themselves in the category of "white," as racial and ethnic issues in Russian are framed differently (where Americans say "white" to distinguish from people of African and Asian descent, Russians say "European"). Unintentionally, by inserting themselves into the story, they have performed a move equivalent to countering "Black Lives Matter" with "All Lives Matter," assuming that issues of racial violence should be understood in a non-racial context.

One of Nadya's next videos, "Make America Great Again" (October 27, 2016) looks designed to neutralize this kind of criticism. A warning about what might happen if Trump were to win the upcoming presidential election, its lyrics call for "letting other people in," and to "stop killing black children." This time, little effort is made to connect the American situation to that of Russia. Once more, though, it is Nadya's body that is the object of the abuse and torture meted out by the forces of injustice (in this case, the police in Trump's America). Nadya also plays one of the cops, not to mention Donald Trump. Once again, she is playing with her own glamour, striking sexy poses in some shots while exposing her body to literally graphic abuse in others (the police officers use a hot brand to burn epithets onto her body). Though localizing the injustice in America this time, Nadya is still using her own body as a universal recipient of abuse, a voodoo doll of state torture.

This makes for an occasionally uncomfortable viewing experience, which is presumably intentional. But there are also times when her body and the motivation for abuse are mismatched. At one point, she is stripped to her underwear and stood before a diagram of the "perfect" women's body. That body doesn't look like Nadya's but it is difficult to see her as a model of bodily diversity when she looks so much like a model. The police even brand her with the words "FAT PIG," which, rather than reinforcing a message of body positivity, is simply puzzling.

The clip ends with Nadya zipped up in a body bag. It's a powerful image, but it's also striking that a self-consciously feminist artist is availing herself of the time-worn trope of the woman's beautiful corpse.[7]

Nadya has produced several other clips under the Pussy Riot name, including one called "Police State," co-starring Chloe Sevigny, "Organs" (a slow rap about the police state, featuring a naked Nadya covered in blood in a bathtub), and "Straight Outta Vagina," a feminist anthem that reminds misogynists where they actually came from (even if it does beg the question of Caesarian sections).

Nadya has also published two books, the first one a collection of her prison correspondence with the Slovenian philosopher Slavoj Zizek, and the second, *Read and Riot: A Pussy Riot Guide to Activism,* which is both a how-to book for aspiring protesters, activists, and proponents of direct democracy, as well as a first-person memoir tracing her life before, during, and after Pussy Riot. Though the cover shows a woman in a balaclava, that woman is clearly meant to be Nadya. In some of her videos, she alternates between her old balaclava and her now-famous, unmasked visage ("Police State" shows her being forcibly unmasked). At this point, Nadya seems quite comfortable being the face of Pussy Riot, whether behind the balaclava or in front of the camera.

As these last videos suggest, she and Masha do not appear together anymore. In the first months after their time in prison, they traveled throughout the country; on one occasion, they were sprayed with a green liquid by counter protesters. They were also among the masked Pussy Rioters who protested the Sochi Olympics, only to be whipped by Cossacks (an event more anachronistic and postmodern than anything Pussy Riot itself could have planned). Equally jarring was their decision to appear on an episode of the Netflix drama *House of Cards*—it turns out that they're fans of the show.[8]

Masha published her own book in 2017, entitled *Riot Days: A Memoir of Punk Protest and Activism*, and toured in a theatrical production based on it the previous year. That same year, she toured in the Belarus Free Theater's production of *Burning Doors*, also partly based on her experience while incarcerated. On stage, she took the Pussy Riot motif of bodily vulnerability to an extreme; in each performance, the actor playing a guard dunks her head in a bathtub while she tries to recite a poem.

Inevitably, Masha's and Nadya's personal lives would also become the stuff of media fascination. First there were the reports of a falling out between the two of them (some alleging a love triangle involving Petya), then the news that Nadya and Petya had broken up, although they remained friends and continued to stay in their daughter's life.[9] When four members of Pussy Riot rushed onto the field during the 2018 World Cup in Moscow, Petya was one of them. This was not the first time a man had been involved in a post-Punk-Prayer Pussy Riot action; the Sochi protest also included a man. But the World Cup event included Veronika Nikulshina, his new partner. In an interview with Russian videoblogger Yuri Dud', Nadya insisted that her relationship with both Petya and Nikulshina was cordial (Dud', 2018).

Nadya's and Petya's divorce appears to have been rather undramatic, and was not particularly fertile ground for gossip. Masha, on the other hand, shocked her friends and, eventually, the media, when it was revealed that she was romantically involved with Dmitry Enteo, a young Orthodox activist known for his attacks on "blasphemous" art in general and his demand for a harsh punishment for Pussy Riot in particular. However surprising their romance, they did eventually find common cause politically, co-organizing an art action against torture in front of the secret service building where so many of the victims of Stalin's purges were tortured and killed.[10]

The very fact that it is possible to gossip about Nadya and Masha is an obvious consequence of the end of their anonymity. But what about the members of Pussy Riot who remain anonymous, or who joined (anonymously) in recent years? After Masha, Nadya, and Katya were initially sentenced, anonymous Pussy Riot released a song called "Putin Lights the Fires of Revolution." It is a perfect stylistic match with previous Pussy Riot songs (something that cannot be said of Masha's and Nadya's later work), with the women shouting the lyrics to the accompaniment of electric guitars.

In the previous chapter, we discussed their letter of February 6, 2014, which expressed their happiness that Masha and Nadya were released, as well as their conviction that, precisely because they are now public as "Masha and Nadya," nothing they do from that point on can be considered the work of Pussy Riot. We have also seen that, while Nadya and Masha themselves were initially firm in maintaining a similar position, that distinction has been lost in the years to follow.

Anonymous Pussy Riot maintains a blog on LiveJournal, though it is updated infrequently. That blog is where the February 6, 2014 letter first appeared, under the title, "So listen to us, at last!" On May 22, 2015, they took a much more sarcastic and combative tone in a post entitled "Action! Action! Pussy Riot Liquidation! Pussy Riot Is Dead" (with the last phrase in English, spelled out in Cyrillic letters). It also had a larger, alternate heading, "PUSSY RIOT IS DEAD!" (in English) followed by the Russian sub-header, "Corpses rot, while the worms stay silent."[11] By now, anonymous Pussy Riot is obviously fed up with Masha and Nadya:

A lot of people ask us: what happened to us, now that we're free? Why have we changed? Where did feminism, protest, and so on, go? We can explain: over the past two years our lives have changed dramatically—we've become very popular: now foreigners think of Russia not only in terms of vodka, bears, the Kalashnikov, but also Pussy Riot. We have fans throughout the world, the media follow our every move, people ask for our autograph on the street . . . We've become stars!

They claim to have had a makeover and bought five suitcases full of clothes in order to travel to New York and Miami Beach: "We understand: art is not our market anymore":

According to the Pussy Riot © branding plan, we've started appearing in tv dramas, videos, and photo shoots, giving interviews 24/7 . . . And now we're preparing our merch: office supplies, t-shirts, mugs, keychains, . . . You might be surprised and ask, "But you're not musicians, you can only do self-promotion ("piarit'sia"). How do you plan on winning over our country? After all, we only value real talent?" Our reply: for us, self-promotion (PR) is the real talent of a musician and of any creative person, and accounts for 100% of a successful career.

They explain that since guerilla marketing (i.e., illegal concerts) has worked so well for them before, they'll now be doing unannounced concerts in food courts. Playing on the multiple meanings of the Russian word "aktsiia" ("action"), which, in addition to describing the activist events made famous by Pussy Riot in the past, is also used to denote a sale or promotion at a store, anonymous Pussy Riot posts a video from the food court, with them standing on tables and performing their song "Action! Action! Pussy Riot Liquidation Sale! Pussy Riot Is Dead!"

With verses attacking the traditional targets of Pussy Riot (Putinism, conformity capitalism) and hurling barely concealed barbs at Nadya and Masha (with references to talk shows and the appropriation of balaclavas for a "whorish masquerade"), the song's chorus doubles down on the group's anarchist values:

Action! Action! Success and adaptation!
Action! Action! Commercialization!
Action! Action! Art capitulations!
Action! Action! Self-exploitation! [*Тебя эксплуатация!*]
. . .
Action! Action! Order and fulfillment!
Action! Action! Fast Food and masturbation!
Action! Action! Capitulation!
Action! Action! Plan for administration!

The last variation of the verse ends with the phrase "Action! Action! Putin's castration."

Over the course of the next week, anonymous Pussy Riot continues to make posts about their "Pussy Riot Liquidation Sale." Their approach contains elements of what Russians call *styob*, which Alexei Yurchak defines as a kind of satire through over-identification with its object (like Stephen Colbert's right-wing cable bloviator in his *Daily Show* days). The authors of the posts pretend to be thrilled at the possibilities that selling out might give them.

On Day One, they claim to be having a sale on balaclavas, "which will not only warm you during those cold evenings, but also become an excellent accessory at invitation-only dinner parties."[12] True, they continue, you might have some concerns that the fashion for activism and protest has passed, but "we predict its return in 10–12 years, and by then the *value of the balaclava will have grown tenfold!*" Nor should the purchaser forget about the product's authenticity: "It has spent time in many police precincts, and is soaked with *our sweat and tears!*"

Thus anonymous Pussy Riot makes its opinion of Masha's and Nadya's public activities clear, by pretending to do them one better: embracing the crassest, most commercial deployment of the Pussy Riot "brand," as though they were selling shoes or televisions rather than fighting for social change.

Just two weeks later, they put aside all playful pretense and once again issued a firm statement, this time explicitly condemning Nadya and Masha for issuing a studio album under the name Pussy Riot without asking the post's anonymous authors. Though they were unhappy with the pair for some time now, they had been making allowances for the women's "dramatic experience of life in the prison colony." However:

> ... we hold antiauthoritarian, left feminist positions, and the personal interests of the participants cannot contradict the concept of the group.... The public conduct of Nadezhda Tolokonnikova and Maria Alyokhina makes us blush with shame for the group's name.

> We demand the cessation of exploitation of the image and materials of the group on the part of Masha and Nadya. We want to place particular emphasis on the fact that we do not intend to function as a group in the future. We consider it obvious that the group has exhausted itself as an artistic project and is no longer a viable phenomenon.[13]

This post was on June 8, 2015. An unsympathetic reading of the anonymous Pussy Riot blog would note that they spent well over two weeks explaining, in great detail, that they no longer exist. But that is the downside of anonymity: if people don't know who and where you are, how will they know when you're really gone?

When the group issued what appeared to be truly its last word on its own non-existence, it did so in a way that playfully foreclosed any sequels. While I do not know when the post went live, it is dated "March 4, 2024"; which, given the allusions to the "recent" Pussy Riot "liquidation sale," was probably almost nine years in the future. After talking briefly about their commitment to anonymity, they complain that, in reaction to their "media war" (presumably the "Pussy Riot Is Dead" campaign), they have "lost Internet accounts and followers, and desperately battled an army of bots from Navalny, Kremlin youth group supporters, and your cynical indifference":

> In accordance with our plan, we are ceasing to exist. To history we will remain marginal unknowns, trashy scum who get around all the rules.... Society has so developed its cult of self

promotion that either directly or under the cover of decorative social projects, you are forced to be conformists.

The provocations are over. And the situation has changed so much that there is no longer any need for the group's existence. We take our leave of you. Please leave us alone—the group does not play music, does not dance, does not go on talk shows, does not appear in films and does not charge $50 to talk to people for 15 minutes. The group is dead. The corpses are rotting, and the worms are silent.[14]

The bitterness of anonymous Pussy Riot is understandable, even predictable. Once Katya, Masha, and Nadya were exposed, the path of anonymity was closed to them, leaving two options: exiting the stage (Katya) or turning their unwanted fame into a weapon (Masha and Nadya). The media spotlight could be appropriated for their use, but it would not work if they used it to complain constantly about their lack of anonymity. Hence the stark contrast between ex-Pussy Riot and anonymous Pussy Riot, with the former seeming to enjoy their fame, and the latter disgusted by their former comrades' cooptation. Once Masha and Nadya stopped protesting that they were no longer Pussy Riot, they became, in the eyes of their anonymous sisters, an ill-fitting public mask that could never have the simple purity of the balaclava.

# CONCLUSION: THE PUNK ART OF COMPROMISE

On May 31, 2019, Alexey Yershov was arrested on Red Square. Yershov, the director of the experimental theater company "Theater to Go," had been holding a poster with the words "Against the Stanislavsky Method."

The Stanislavsky Method, one of Russia's most significant contributions to the world of theater, requires actors to delve into the psychological motivations of their characters, and involves a variety of off-script exercises aimed at helping actors master the emotions they are trying to evoke. Yershov and his fellow protesters issued a statement to MediaZona: "In its totalitarianism, the method leads to stagnation. By rejecting the method today, you reject the proposition of existing in the status quo tomorrow (and you might even save an elk)." (Veronika Nikulshina of Pussy Riot protested with the same slogan in Moscow's Elk Forest nature preserve).[1]

Yershov's hostility to the Stanislavsky Method is consistent with the far looser principles of Actionism, but that is hardly the point. In fact, Yershov's protest exposed the vulnerability of Actionism itself in the Russia of 2019. In the old days (less than a decade before), Actionists were staging orgies, vandalizing bridges, and throwing live animals at cashiers. Now all it took to get arrested was holding a placard with an obscure slogan whose connection to politics required extensive footnoting.

Thanks to the harsh laws passed in the wake of the 2011–2012 protest movements (not to mention the Punk Prayer), public protest had become a rarity. When, just a week after Yershov's protest, hundreds of people turned out to protest the arrest of crusading Meduza journalist Ivan Golunov on trumped-up drug charges, the government was taken by surprise: nothing like this had happened in years. Golunov was released, but 500 people were rounded up and arrested (all but four were discharged soon afterwards).[2]

Russia during Putin's third and fourth terms was not a country where protest was treated lightly, and therefore not a place where the decision to take to the streets could be an easy one. Just as the rise of the protest movement and the outrage over electoral fraud were essential contexts for understanding Pussy Riot in 2012, the repressive climate in the years since Nadya's and Masha's release must factor into any consideration of the afterlife of Pussy Riot. As the philosopher Mikhail Ryklin explained in an interview in 2016:

> If such a group were to appear now, it would be immediately crushed by the authorities. Pussy Riot has tried to protest. During the 2014 Olympics they put on an anti-Putinist performance in Sochi. They were beaten. Then they went to Nizhnyi Novgorod to visit a prison colony. They were attacked by a group of people wearing the St. George Ribbon [a symbol used for commemorating those who died in World War II, and adopted by conservative nationalists in the aftermath of the war in Ukraine]
>
> . . .
>
> Now no one can fight with the currently existing regime. There are no such people. Pussy Riot protested in Medvedev's Russia. Medvedev used to say that freedom was better than unfreedom. This was a relatively favorable time for protest.[3]

Ryklin makes an important point, one that must be factored into any consideration of Pussy Riot, Nadya, and Masha since 2014. Anonymous Pussy Riot could perhaps have attempted further actions along the lines of their pre-Punk Prayer performances, but the odds of their arrest and conviction were high. Nadya and Masha faced two additional obstacles: their loss of anonymity made fading into the crowd all but impossible, and their prior conviction guaranteed a harsh sentence.

In the history of dissidence and protest, there have been people who are willing to be arrested and re-arrested, at the risk of spending most of their lives in confinement: Nelson Mandela in South Africa, Aung San Suu Kyi in Myanmar (Burma), and Andrei Sakharov in the Soviet Union, to name just a few. Their commitment and sacrifice demand respect, but their number has always been few.

Nadya and Masha could have chosen that path, but they did not. Can anyone honestly blame them? To be disappointed in them for declining to engage in total self-sacrifice is a morally dubious proposition. Working safely and comfortably in my office in New York City, I certainly have no standing to criticize them for their apparent unwillingness to spend the rest of their lives in a Russian penal colony. Nor am I inclined to do so.

The same holds true for Katya, who retreated into private life not long after narrowly escaping the same sentence as Masha and Nadya. In fact, her decision has proved much more straightforward than those of her former partners in "crime," since her path has amounted to choosing between being a public or a private person. This decision, once made, quickly forecloses any extended discussion. She is no longer the focus of people's aspirations for political change, or the target of ongoing opprobrium. Articles on Katya still occasionally pop up in the media, but mostly in the "Where are they now?" genre.[4]

In their refusal to remain silent, as well as in their choices of new projects and their apparent willingness to exploit the Pussy Riot brand, Masha and Nadya continue to make choices in public, and therefore continue to be subject to scrutiny and criticism (as well as admiration). Assessing their post-prison activities, more often than not, is wrapped up with one's understanding of who and what they were before their arrest. Are they a punk band who have sold out? Radical feminists who exploit their appearance? Anarchists who have gone commercial? Young rebels who have grown into mature dissidents?

There is a pop culture master plot that helps us understand Masha's and Nadya's life after Pussy Riot, one briefly invoked in the discussion of anonymity in Chapter 10. The balaclava-clad Pussy Riot repeatedly compared themselves to superheroes. There are reasons some superheroes choose to wear masks, primarily involving the freedom of action available to them when their identity is concealed. Just as unmasking would mean the end of a vigilante such as Batman, it rendered the continuation of Nadya's and Masha's masked Pussy Riot activities impossible. Without their balaclavas to disguise them, Nadya and Masha had no choice but to find another way to pursue their activist agendas.

Nadya seems to point towards one possible interpretation with the tragically un-hip assertion discussed in the last chapter ("The real punk is to build institutions"). On the face of it, this is simply laughable: as much as one might admire the hard-working policy wonks and technocrats of *Parks and Recreation* or *The West Wing* (not to mention their real-life counterparts), they are anything but punk. Instead, it looks as though Nadya is saying that anything she does is punk by definition, or that, as one of the most famous figures associated with punk today, she is the final arbiter of what is punk and what is not.

But perhaps this is too literal an understanding of "punk" as Nadya is using it, and too narrow an approach to what Pussy Riot was actually about. The most obvious criticisms of Nadya in particular upon release were about appearance, image, and style (in the case of the fashion shoot, quite literally so). Even during the trial itself, the three defendants made no effort to maintain their punk anarchist personae when finally given the chance to speak. Again, this is a matter of form, rather than content. As we saw in Chapter 6, the arguments Katya, Nadya, and Masha put forth were entirely consistent with the public ethos of Pussy Riot, but presented in a logically persuasive, intelligent manner. They did not spend their precious few moments at the podium shouting "Putin has pissed himself!", but they maintained the political positions evident in their songs.

Upon their release, they did not, initially, devote themselves to music or activism, but chose to establish Zona Prava and MediaZona, institutions designed to expose corruption and (re)build civil society in their home country. When they did return to the stage and screen, it was with performances whose musical and visual aesthetic had little in common with earlier Pussy Riot. And, of course, they toured the world and appeared on *House of Cards* and *The Colbert Report*. How is this punk rather than simply selling out?

If we take a long view of the activities of the no-longer-anonymous women of Pussy Riot, we are reminded that their adoption of punk was more fortuitous than planned. It was not a matter of a life-long dream of becoming musicians, or a total commitment to punk music. Punk was a mantle they put on when looking for a feminist next step after Voina. It was only a lifestyle choice to the extent that the punk aesthetic and mythology of 1970s punk dovetailed with Actionism, political anarchism, and feminism.

This book is subtitled "Speaking Punk to Power" not only to highlight the standoff between Pussy Riot and the state, but to suggest an approach to punk that is less about identity than it is about a performance or a set of speech acts. For Nadya and Masha, at least, punk was a means to an end. That end was not global fame; global fame is yet another means. The goal has always been political and social change.

While this is surely the case for Nadya, it is even more obviously so for Masha. Before her involvement with Voina and Pussy Riot, Masha was involved in environmental activism.[5] Nadya's politics, as she presents them in her interviews and her books, seem to come from personal experience and character combined with intellectual and philosophical study. But both of them, whether through art, protest, institution building, or some combination of all three, are committed to transforming the world in which they live.

At the same time, the world has also transformed them. This is an obvious point, and should be expected, but it is worth remembering. The women of Pussy Riot were quite young when the group began; they essentially spent their twenties in the public eye. The fact that they may have changed in some way should be less shocking than the possibility that they have not.

Their experience and behavior in court, prison, and upon release demonstrate both a step away from punk as form and a continuation of the impulse behind their punk years. Consternation at some of their videos, or at their apparent growing comfort with their celebrity, makes some sense, but it should also remind us of the media's fundamental failure to understand Pussy Riot from the very beginning, trying to pigeonhole them as a band, or even, occasionally, as a feminist guerrilla cell. The media have continually wanted them to be one thing, or at least one thing at a time.

But the women of Pussy Riot have always been reactive in the best sense; that is, they adapt to circumstance and change their tactics and aesthetic approach when necessary. They are improvisers who work with the material at hand. In recent years, that material has included fame.

As they move further into institution-building and further into their thirties, Masha and Nadya are consistent in their inconsistencies. They are also growing into their roles, or, to use a word that is unavoidably condescending, growing up.

Growing up does not have to mean selling out. There is a less binary model available for understanding Nadya's and Masha's development, and it points to perhaps the least punk art form imaginable: socialist realism, the official art of the Soviet Union starting in 1932.

As Katerina Clark persuasively demonstrates in *The Soviet Novel: History as Ritual*, the master plot of socialist realism recapitulates the Leninist dialectic of spontaneity and consciousness.[6] In simpler terms, it is about the tensions between impulsive, well-meaning activism and slow, sometimes inertly bureaucratic, systemic thought. The hero of socialist realism is on the "correct" side (that of Soviet state socialism), but is unwilling to submit to the rigid strictures of the Party when he (usually "he") sees a problem to be solved or a challenge to be met. Disregarding his superiors who tell him his plans are impractical, he forges ahead. Along the way, he usually consults with a mentor, whose advice pushes him further in the direction of consciousness (the system) even as he follows his impulses to successfully implement change. By the end of the story, he has achieved his goal, usually at the cost of some terrible sacrifice—on the one hand proving the need for people such as himself while on the other, now willingly incorporating himself within the system that he had previously seen as an obstacle.

Clark's argument is about socialist realism, though she does bring in other mass art from the West towards the end of her study. But what she has discovered is far broader than her book's claim: this master plot functions independent of Party or state strictures as the dynamic underlying most popular narratives of activism, resistance, and social change. In American film and televisions, this is usually the story of one person (often a woman), who discovers an injustice that affects her personally (environmental poisoning, harassment at work, the scheming of oppressive insurance companies). With little background in politics, she finds herself engaged in activism, and teaching herself about politics along the way, both through meeting a mentor, and through independent research, usually shown in scenes of her sitting up late at night, massaging her eyes while looking at a computer screen or a stack of books, as empty pizza boxes pile up around her. By the end of the film, she may have won her case, or perhaps even lost it, but by now she is part of a broader movement, one that she has either founded or expanded through her own participation.

The appeal of this model is precisely that it is a dialectic rather than a simple binary: both spontaneity and consciousness are necessary, and the transformation of an individual crusader into a movement activist (or Party member) reflects the growing maturity of the individual while also recognizing the crucial role played by the non-systemic outsider in refreshing the system and furthering its goals.

In certain obvious ways, this model does not reflect the experience of Masha and Nadya. To claim that they were in some way not politically "conscious" or were ideologically naive before their arrest would be insulting. But when we recall the critique of Pussy Riot by movement feminists in Chapter 9, or even by Maria Arbatova, as we look at Nadya's and Masha's activities today, we see two activists who followed their ideals and, along the way, learned more about the system that oppressed not just them, but, more important, millions of people who would never have their access to the spotlight. Their trial and imprisonment were a crash course in the Russian penal system and the Russian media; when they rejoined public life, they took what they learned and made it the central objects of their post-imprisonment activism (Zona prava and MediaZona). They built institutions.

Does this mean they are no longer punk? Not if you agree with Nadya's words on the matter. If "punk" represents the non-systemic, wildly unconventional activism of Pussy Riot, then the dialectic approach suggests that, in joining and building institutions, Masha and Nadya reinvigorate them with the primal energy of punk, even if some of their time ends up spent on mission statements and board meetings.

It's the same fight, but with different weapons.

# NOTES

## Introduction

1. Thomas Grove, "New Russian video game takes aim at punk band riot," Reuters, July 11, 2013. https://www.reuters.com/article/us-russia-pussyriot-videogame/new-russian-video-game-takes-aim-at-punk-band-riot-idUSBRE96A0VY20130711

2. Natalya Krainova, "One Pussy Riot Member Freed by Moscow Court," *The Moscow Times*, October 9, 2012. https://www.themoscowtimes.com/2012/10/09/one-pussy-riot-member-freed-by-moscow-court-a18461

3. Scott Neuman, "Pussy Riot's Pyotr Verzilov, Allegedly Poisoned, is Flown to Germany for Treatment," NPR, September 17, 2018. https://www.npr.org/2018/09/17/648645607/pussy-riots-pyotr-verzilov-allegedly-poisoned-is-flown-to-germany-for-treatment

4. Jillian Rayfield, "Obama: The 80s called, they want their foreign policy back." Salon October 23, 2012. https://www.salon.com/2012/10/23/obama_the_80s_called_they_want_their_foreign_policy_back/

5. For an overview of Perestroika and the 1990s, see Stephen Kotkin, *Armageddon Averted: The Soviet Collapse, 1970–2000* (Oxford: Oxford University Press, 2008).

6. For divergent overviews of Russia under Putin, see Karen Dawisha, *Putin's Kleptocracy: Who Owns Russia?* (New York: Simon & Schuster, 2015); Mark Galeotti, *We Need to Talk About Putin: Why the West Gets Him Wrong, and How to Get Him Right* (New York: Ebury Press, 2019); Masha Gessen, *The Man Without a Face: The Unlikely Rise of Vladimir Putin* (New York: Riverhead Books, 2012); Shaun Walker, *The Long Hangover: Putin's New Russia and the Ghosts of the Past* ( Oxford: Oxford University Press, 2019); and Mikhail Zygar, *All the Kremlin's Men: Inside the Court of Vladimir Putin* (New York: PublicAffairs, 2017).

7. Max Atkinson (trans.), "First English Translation of Putin's Victory Speech," *Huffington Post*, March 7, 2012. https://www.huffingtonpost.co.uk/max-atkinson/first-english-translation_b_1324966.html

8. The protests of 2012 and 2013 garnered a great deal of international media attention at the time, and have already produced excellent scholarly literature. An excellent place to start is Mischa Gabowitsch, *Protest in Putin's Russia* (New York: Polity, 2017), followed by Birgit Beumers,

Alexander Etkind, Olga Gurov, and Sanna Turoma (eds), *Cultural Forms of Protest in Russia* (New York: Routledge, 2017).

9. Tom Breihan, "Pussy Riot Face Dumb Questions, Prudish Reporters in Post-Prison Media Frenzy," *Sterogum*, 2013. http://www.stereogum.com/1614372/pussy-riot-face-dumb-questions-prudish-reporters-in-post-prison-media-frenzy/video/

10. Rebecca Rose, "Amy Schumer Bravely Won the Right to Say 'Pussy' on Comedy Central," *Jezebel*, November 9, 2014. https://jezebel.com/amy-schumer-bravely-won-the-right-to-say-pussy-on-comed-1656702945

11. "Interview to Russia Today TV Channel" 2012.

12. Eve Ensler, *The Vagina Monologues* (New York: Random House, 2001); Inga Muscio, *Cunt: A Declaration of Independence* (Berkeley: Seal Press, 2012).

13. Mikhail Iampolskii makes a similar point: Actionism "violates the barriers between politics, art, and sexuality. These border violations have so become the norm that the very question of distinctly assigning this or that gesture to the category of politics, the body, or art seems meaningless. And blurring these boundaries, as Pussy Riot has shown, has a truly explosive effect": Mikhail Iampol'skii, "Tri sloia testa na odnu izvilinu vlasti," *Novoe vremia*, August 20, 2012. https://newtimes.ru/articles/detail/55977

## Chapter 1

1. Nikolai Troitskii, "Stilisticheskii dissident Andrei Siniavskii," RIA Novosti, October 8, 2010. https://ria.ru/20101008/283408447.html

2. There is a large and growing body of English-language scholarship on Moscow Conceptualism and the figures associated with it. See Keti Chukhrov, "Soviet Material Culture and Socialist Ethics in Moscow Conceptualism. Conceptual Artwork as an Index Machine," *e-flux* 29 (November 2011). https://www.e-flux.com/journal/29/68089/soviet-material-culture-and-socialist-ethics-in-moscow-conceptualism/3; Mikhail Epstein, *After the Future: The Paradoxes of Postmodernism and Contemporary Russian Culture* (Amherst: University of Massachusetts Press, 1995); Boris Groys, *The Total Art of Stalinism: Avant-garde, Aesthetic Dictatorship, and Beyond* (New York: Verso, 2014); Matthew Jesse Jackson, *The Experimental Group: Ilya Kabakov, Moscow Conceptualism, Soviet Avant-Garde* (Chicago: University of College, 2010); Gerald Janecek, *Everything Has Already Been Written: Moscow Conceptualist Poetry and*

*Performance* (Evanston: Northwestern University Press, 2018); Daniil Leiderman, "The Strategy of Shimmering in Moscow Conceptualism," *Russian Literature* 96–98 (February, 2018): 51–76; Mark Lipovetsky, "Pussy Riot as the Trickstar," *Postmodern Crises: From "Lolita" to Pussy Riot* (Boston: Academic Studies Press, 2017); and Larissa Rudova, "Paradigms of Postmodernism: Conceptualism and Sots-Art in Contemporary Russian Literature," *Pacific Coast Philology* 35.1 (2000): 61–75.

3. For a highly readable overview of the Situationist International, see McKenzie Wark, *The Beach Beneath the Street: The Everyday Life and Glorious Times of the Situationist International* (New York: Verso, 2015).

4. Pussy Riot is also linked to the Situationists by virtue of the mere fact of their cathedral performance, which echoes a similar action by the Situationists' immediate precursors, the Lettrists; on April 9, 1950, the Lettrists interrupted a mass at Notre Dame in order to declaim their own anti-sermon on the death of God. The mass was being broadcast live.

5. For more on Viennese Actionism, see Hubert Klocker, *Rite of Passage: The Early Years of Vienna Actionism 1960–1966* (Gent: Snoeck, 2014) and Mechtild Widrich, "The Informative Public of Performance. A Study of Viennese Actionism," *TDR. The Drama Review* 1 (Spring 2013): 137–151.

6. On Moscow Actionism, see Herwig G Höller, "Moscow Actionism: Origins and Applications," *Springerin* 2 (2003). https://www.springerin.at/en/2003/2/moskauer-aktionismen-ursprunge-und-verwendungen/; Sasha Raspopina, "Beyond Pussy Riot: 7 Controversial Actionist-Artists You Should Know, *The Calvert Journal*, November 27, 2017; and Nele Sasz, "'Radical' Art in Russia, the 1990s and Beyond," Artmargins, June 11, 2003. https://artmargins.com/qradicalq-art-in-russia-the-1990s-and-beyond/.

7. For a thorough history and analysis of Voina, see Alek Epshtein, *Total'naia "Voina." Art-aktivizm epokhi tandemokratii* (Moscow: Umlaut, 2012).

8. "Voina: Fuck for the Heir Puppy Bear At II (2008). https://www.youtube.com/watch?v=JnBC4PRAdLM&list=PLCYnWz2M3_U9CmPDmmxD6T3shUMzibNuI.

9. Valerie Sperling, *Sex, Politics, and Putin: Political Legitimacy in Russia* (Oxford: Oxford University Press, 2014), 16–19.

10. The Women in Black are an international peace movement that began in Israel in 1988. They gather for silent vigils in protest of war and violence, and, as their name suggests, they wear black.

11. "Prikoly: Kak urkast' kuritsu – master-klass ot gruppy Voina." June 29, 2010. http://video.bigmir.net/show/150785/

## Notes

12. Valerii Pecheikin, "Lobzai musora," *Kvir* 94 (April, 2011). https://wisegizmo. livejournal.com/54844.html

13. Sperling (2014), 228.

14. Pecheikin (2011).

15. Masha Gessen, *Words Will Break Cement: The Passion of Pussy Riot* (New York: Riverhead Books, 2014), 60.

## Chapter 2

1. Elena Zdravomyslova and Anna Temkina, "The Crisis of Masculinity in Late Soviet Discourse," *Russian Studies in History* 51.2 (2014): 13–34.

2. "Pussy Riot -Kill the Sexist!" 2012. https://www.youtube.com/ watch?v=cNznbWQmXnY

3. Masha Gessen, *Words Will Break Cement: The Passion of Pussy Riot* (New York: Riverhead Books, 2014), 64.

4. Nadya Tolokonnikova, *Read and Riot: A Pussy Riot Guide to Activism* (New York: HarperOne, 2018), 68.

5. "Priamaia liniia s Tolokonnikovoi i Alekhinoi: o Khodorkovskom, Putine i novom proekte. Polnaia versiia. Chast' 1," (2013). TV Rain, December 27, 2103. https://tvrain.ru/lite/teleshow/experiment/prjamaja_linija_s_ tolokonnikovoj_i_alehinoj_o_hodorkovskom_putine_i_novom_proekte_ polnaja_versija_chast_1-359653/

6. Pussy Riot, "Putin zassal!" [Putin pissed himself], August 16, 2012. https:// www.youtube.com/watch?v=s_bnb8hepds

## Chapter 3

1. Ekaterina V. Haskins, "Russia's Postcommunist Past: The Cathedral of Christ the Savior and the Reimagining of National Identity," *History & Memory* 21.1 (Spring/Summer 2009).

2. Tsereteli is a sculptor who has been president of the Russian Academy of Sciences since 1997, and is best known for his monumental projects, such as a 94-meter high statue of Peter the Great in Moscow.

3. S. M. Kirov, *Izbrannye stat'i i rechi 1912–1934* (Gosudarstvennoe izdatel'stvo politcheskoi literature, 1939), 29.

4. Haskins (2009).

## Chapter 4

1. "Pussy Riot – Punk Prayer 'Virgin Mary, Put Putin Away' (English Subtitles)." August 17, 2012. https://www.youtube.com/watch?v=lPDkJbTQRCY

2. Elena Masiuk, "Sviashchennik Gleb Iakunin: Patriarkh Kirill funktsiiu vzial kak by na sebia," *Novaia gazeta*, January 24, 2014. https://www.novayagazeta.ru/articles/2014/01/24/58082-svyaschennik-gleb-yakunin-patriarh-kirill-funktsiyu-kgb-vzyal-kak-by-na-sebya

3. Elena Gapova, "Becoming Visible in The Digital Age: The Class and Media Dimensions of the Pussy Riot Affair," *Feminist Media Studies* 15.1 (2015): 18–35.

4. Sophia Kishkovskynov, "In Russian Chill, Waiting Hours for Touch of the Holy." *New York Times*, November 24, 2011. https://www.nytimes.com/2011/11/24/world/europe/virgin-mary-belt-relic-draws-crowds-in-moscow.html

5. Gleb Bryanski, "Russian patriarch calls Putin era 'miracle of God.'" Reuters. February 8, 2012. https://uk.reuters.com/article/uk-russia-putin-religion/russian-patriarch-calls-putin-era-miracle-of-god-idUKTRE81722Y20120208

## Chapter 5

1. Eliot Borenstein, *Plots against Russia: Conspiracy and Fantasy after Socialism* (Ithaca: Cornell University Press, 2019), 133–144.

2. Elena Gapova, "Delo 'Pusy Riot': feministskij protest v kontekste klassovoj bor'by," *Neprikosnovennyi zapas* 85 (May 2013); Mikhail Epstein, "Minimal Religion," in *Russian Postmodernism: New Perspectives on Post-Soviet Culture*, Mikhail N. Epstein, Alexander A. Genis, and Slobodanka M. Vladiv-Glover (New York: Berghan Books, 1999), 163–171.

3. Anya Bernstein, "An Inadvertent Sacrifice: Body Politics and Sovereign Power in the Pussy Riot Affair," *Critical Inquiry* 40.1 220–241. https://criticalinquiry.uchicago.edu/an_inadvertent_sacrifice_body_politics_and_sovereign_power_in_the_pussy_rio/

4. In addition to the scholarship on the holy fool in general (Priscilla Hunt and Svitlana Kobets (eds) *Holy Foolishness in Russia. New Perspectives* (Bloomington: Slavica Publishers, 2011); Sergey A. Ivanov, *Holy Fools in Byzantium and Beyond* (Oxford: Oxford University Press, 2006), there is a significant amount of scholarly literature and editorial writing connecting

the holy fool with Pussy Riot. For the latter, see Anna Arutunyan, "Fool. Fool. Holy Fool. How Pussy Riot Is Turning the Government into a Villain and a Crutch," *The Moscow News*, February 4, 2013; Alesha Belochkin, "Farisei i iurodivye," *Novaia gazeta*, March 5, 2012; Viktor Osipov, "Pogranichnyie stolknoveniia," *Izvestiia*, March 16, 2012; Peter Rutland, "What Links Pussy Riot With Dostoevsky," *Moscow Times*, August 27, 2012. For scholarly studies, see Ania Aizman, "The Poor Rhymes of Hooligans: The Anarchist Aesthetics of OBERIU and Pussy Riot" *The Russian Review* 78 (January 2019): 45–61; Nicholas Denysenko "An Appeal to Mary: An Analysis of Pussy Riot's Punk Performance in Moscow," *Journal of the American Academy of Religion* 81.4 (2013): 1061–1092; and Irina Dzero and Tatyana Bystrova, "Pussy Riot and the Translatability of Cultures," *Transcultural Studies* 13.2 (2017): 264–286. For a fascinating hybrid of the two, see Elena Volkova, "PUSSY RIOT SCHOOL. Urok 7. Videniia Marii," November 18, 2012, http://grani.ru/blogs/free/entries/208819.html, for her multi-part mediations on the Pussy Riot phenomenon under the heading "Pussy Riot School."

5. Ivanov (2006), 1.

## Chapter 6

1. Nancy Ries, *Russian Talk: Culture and Conversation during Perestroika* (Ithaca: Cornell University Press, 1997), 84–99.

2. Alexei Yurchak, *Everything Was Forever, Until It Was No More: The Last Soviet Generation* (Princeton: Princeton University Press, 2005), 106–114.

3. In his 1978 essay "The Power of the Powerless," Havel proposes that the best available way to live in a totalitarian system is to "live in truth." The state may constantly lie, surrounding the individual with bombastic propaganda, but the individual can, in their daily life, refuse to assent to the state's lies: Vaclav Havel, *The Power of the Powerless: Citizens Against the State in Central Eastern Europe* (New York: Routledge, 1985). See Jonathan Bolton, *Words of Dissent: Charter 77, the Plastic People of the Universe, and Czech Culture under Communism* (Cambridge MA: Harvard University Press, 2014). Nadya read this essay in prison, and was profoundly moved by it (Tolokonnikova, 2018, 8–9).

4. Mariia Makeeva, "Kofe-breik: Novaia aktsiia v XXS. Balaklavy sdelali iz ikeevskikh navolochek," *TV Rain'* (2013). http://tvrain.ru/teleshow/ coffee_break/novaja_aktsija_v_hhs_balaklavy_sdelali_iz_ikeevskih_ navolochek-337214/.

5. Sergei Oushakine argues that the dissident writings in late Soviet times was characterized by a "terrifying mimicry" of the official discourse, a function of the "dissidents' attempt to experience the dominant discourse not only as *acting on* them but also as *activating and forming* their subjectivity": Serguei Oushakine, "The Terrifying Mimicry of Samizdat," *Public Culture* 13.2 (2001): 191–214.

6. Mischa Gabowitsch, "Are Copycats Subversive? Strategy-31, the Russian Runs, the Immortal Regiment, and the Transformative Potential of Non-hierarchical Movements," in *Cultural Forms of Protest in Russia*, ed. Birgit Beumers, Alexander Etkind, Olga Gurov, and Sanna Turoma (New York: Routledge, 2017): 68–89.

7. Masha Gessen, *Words Will Break Cement: The Passion of Pussy Riot* (New York: Riverhead Books, 2014), 170.

8. Marijeta Bozovic Maria Corrigan, Chto Delat, Elena Glazov-Corrigan, Maksim Hanukai, Katharine Holt, Ainsley Morse, and Sasha Senderovich, "Pussy Riot: Translators' Statements," *N+1*. August 13, 2012.

9. All three closing statements are quoted from the English translations published on the website for the magazine N+1. Katya's statement was translated by Cho Delat News, Masha's by Marijeta Bozovic, Maksim Hanukai, and Sasha Senderovich. Nadya's was translated by Maria Corrigan and Elena Glazov-Corrigan.

## Chapter 7

1. For more on Pavlensky, see Vladimir D. Mendelevich, "The Extraordinary Case of Russian Performance Artist Pyotr Pavlensky: Psychopathology or Contemporary Art?" *Transcultural Psychiatry* 56.3 (June 2018): 569–585; Ingrid Nelson, "Artist for a New Age: Dissident Russian Performance Art and the Work of Petr Pavlenskii," *Russian Literature* 96–98 (2018): 277–295; and Jonathan Brooks Platt, "Hysteria or Enjoyment? Recent Russian Actionism," In *Cultural Forms of Protest in Russia*, ed. Birgit Beumers, Alexander Etkind, Olga Gurov, and Sanna Turoma (New York: Routledge, 2017), 141–159.

2. Henry Langston, "Meeting Pussy Riot. Putin's Put Them in Prison Now, but We Spoke to Them back in February," *Vice*, March 10, 2012. https://www.vice.com/en_uk/article/kwnzgy/A-Russian-Pussy-Riot.

3. Elena Masiuk, "Nadezhda Tolokonnikova My nevol'no stali epitsentrom bol'shogo politicheskogo sobytiia," *Novaia gazeta*. August 20, 2012.

## Notes

4. Arkadii Mamontov, "Spetsial'nyi korrespondent. Sodom," May 27, 2015. https://www.youtube.com/watch?v=3oIVr7jW_SI

5. Arkadii Mamontov, "Spetsial'nyi korrespondent. Provokatory." https://www.youtube.com/watch?v=-yk4lLQ_9Hg

6. Arkadii Mamontov, "Spetsial'nyi korrespondent. Provokatory." https://www.youtube.com/watch?v=-yk4lLQ_9Hg

7. Arkadii Mamontov, *Provokatory-2*. September 11, 2012. https://www.youtube.com/watch?v=z0oHHEtcMdM

8. Kseniia Sobchak, and Kseniia Sokolova, "Ekaterina Samutsevich. Neraschekhlennaia." *Snob* (2012). http://snob.ru/selected/entry/53946.

9. Ilya Yablokok, Fortress Russia: Conspiracy Theories in the Post-Soviet World (New York: Polity, 2018), 112–131.

10. Arkadii Mamontov, "Spetsial'nyi korrespondent. Provokatory 3." https://www.youtube.com/watch?v=dnTjEpSBMdI

## Chapter 8

1. The centrality of presence is a subject of continued debate in performance art circles. The touchstone is the work of Philip Auslander, exemplified by his book *Liveness: Performance in Mediatized Culture* (New York: Routledge, 2008). The question is addressed by performers as well as scholars (Jen Ortiz, "Can Performance Art be Collected . . . and Still Maintain its Original Message . . .?" *Hyperallergic*, June 28, 2012. https://hyperallergic.com/53624/can-performance-art-be-collected). See also Baz Kershaw, "Performance as Research: Live Events and Documents," in *Cambridge Companion to Performance Studies*, ed. Tracy C. Davis (Cambridge: Cambridge University Press, 2098), 23–45 and Richard Schechner, *Performance Theory* (New York: Routledge, 2004), and *Performance Studies: An Introduction,* 3rd edn (New York: Routledge, 2017).

2. RoseLee Goldberg, *Performance Art: From Futurism to the Present*, 3rd edn (London: Thames & Hudson, 2011).

3. Tolokonnikova (2018), 68.

4. https://marinaabramovicmademecry.tumblr.com/

5. Rosie Gray, "Pippin Barr, Man Behind the Marina Abramovic Video Game, Weighs In on his Creation," *Village Voice*, September 16, 2011. https://www.villagevoice.com/2011/09/16/pippin-barr-man-behind-the-marina-abramovic-video-game-weighs-in-on-his-creation/

## Chapter 9

1. Richard Stites, *The Women's Liberation Movement in Russia: Feminism, Nihilsm, and Bolshevism, 1860–1930* (Princeton: Princeton University Press, 1979).

2. For the history of homosexuality in the Soviet Union, see Dan Healey, *Homosexual Desire in Revolutionary Russia: The Regulation of Sexual and Gender Dissent* (Chicago: University of Chicago Press, 2001), and *Russian Homophobia from Stalin to* Sochi (London: Bloomsbury, 2017); and Francesca Stella, *Lesbian Lives in Soviet and Post-Soviet Russia Post/ Socialism and Gendered Sexualities* (New York: Palgrave, 2015).

3. Elena Zdravomyslova and Anna Temkina, "The Crisis of Masculinity in Late Soviet Discourse," *Russian Studies in History* 51.2 (2012): 13–34.

4. Borenstein (2019), 136–144.

5. After the collapse of the Soviet Union, the new constitution for the Russian Federation guaranteed freedom of conscience. But the sheer range of religious pluralism was an unforeseen consequence of liberalization, leading to a great deal of public anxiety over new religious movements ("cults). See Oxana Antic, "The Spread of Modern Cults in the USSR," in *Religious Policy in the Soviet Union*, ed. Sabrina Petra Ramet (Cambridge: Cambridge University Press, 1993), 260–261; Eliot Borenstein, "Suspending Disbelief: 'Cults' and Postmodernism in Post-Soviet Russia," in *Consuming Russia*, ed. Adele Barker (Duke University Press, 1999), 437–462; Alexander A. Panchenko, "Morality, Utopia, Discipline: New Religious Movements and Soviet Culture," in *Multiple Moralities and Religions in Post-Soviet Russia*, ed. Jarrett Zigon (New York: Berghahn Books, 2013). Moreover, officials in the Russian Orthodox Church expressed their dismay that Western Protestants looked at the Russian Federation as land ripe for conversion to Christianity, even though the country has Christian roots going back to 1088. The 1997 Law on Freedom of Conscience and Religious Associations recognized the historical status of Judaism, Islam, Buddhism, and the Russian Orthodox Church, establishing a registration regime and various categories for other faith communities that wished to operate on Russian territory. A law in 2006 made registration significantly more difficult, and increased the restrictions on any religious movement that was not one of the four main ones codified in the 1997 Law. See Zoe Knox, "Religious Freedom in Russia: The Putin Years," in *Religion, Morality, and Community in Post-Soviet Societies*, ed. Mark D. Steinberg and Catherine R. Wanner (Bloomington: Indiana University Press, 2008); Roman Lunkin, "The Status of and Challenges to Religious Freedom in Russia," in *The Future of Religious Freedom: Global Challenges,* ed. Allen D. Hertzke (Oxford: Oxford University Press, 2013),

157–180. On the ties between the American religious Right and Russian conservative movements, see Masha Gessen, "Family Values: Mapping the Spread of Antigay Ideology," *Harper's Magazine* (March 2017): 35–40; and Hannah Levintova, "These US Evangelicals Helped Create Russia's Anti-Gay Movement," *Mother Jones* (February 2014).

6. Kevin Moss, "Russia as the Saviour of European Civilization: Gender and the Geopolitics of Traditional Values," in *Anti-Gender Campaigns in Europe: Mobilizing against Equality*, ed. Roman Kuhar and David Paternotte (London: Rowan & Littlefield, 2017), 195–214.

7. For examples of the growing scholarship on the international campaigns against "gender ideology," see Heinrich Boll Foundation (eds), *Anti-Gender Movements on the Rise? Strategizing for Gender Equality in Central and Eastern Europe* , Heinrich Bollstiftung Publication Series on Democracy, no. 38 (2015); Eszter Kovats and Maari Poim (eds), *Gender as Symbolic Glue: The Position and Role of Conservative and Far Right Parties in the Anti-Gender Mobilizations in Europe*, Foundation for European Progressive Studies (2015); Roman Kuhar and David Paternotte (eds), *Anti-Gender Campaigns in Europe: Mobilizing against Equality* (London: Rowan & Littlefield, 2017); and Conor O'Dwyer, *Coming Out of Communism: The Emergence of LGBT Activism in Eastern Europe* (New York: New York University, 2018).

8. "Poslanie prezidenta Federal'nomu sobraniiu," Kremlin.ru. December 12, 2012. www.kremlin.ru/events/president/news/17118

9. Sperling (2014), 225–230.

10. Sperling (2014), 227.

11. (Stites 1979).

12. "Sobchak zhiv'em. Mariia Arbatova," March 7, 2013. http://ksenia-sobchak.com/sobchak-zhivem-mariya-arbatova

13. Elena Stishova, "Masha Arbatova: 'U menia tri erogennye zony – moi deti, muzhchiny i prava cheloveka.'" *Iskusstvo Kino* 5 (April 1997). http://old.kinoart.ru/archive/1997/05/n5-article1

14. Kseniia Sobchak, and Kseniia Sokolova, "Ekaterina Samutsevich. Neraschekhlennaia." *Snob* (2012). http://snob.ru/selected/entry/53946

15. Kseniia Sobchak, "Kto takaia Ekaterina Samutsevich," *Snob* (2012). http://www.snob.ru/profile/24691/blog/53948

16. Kseniia Sobchak, "Tolokonnikova: 'Vystuplenie v khrame bylo oshibkoi.' Alekhina: 'Net, ne beylo.' Interviiu Ksenii Sobchak," *Sobchak zhiv'em*, December 25, 2013. https://tvrain.ru/teleshow/sobchak_zhivem/tolokonnikova_vystuplenie_v_hrame_bylo_oshibkoj_alehina_net_ne_bylo_intervju_ksenii_sobchak_chast_1-359528/

17. Tom Breihan, "Pussy Riot Face Dumb Questions, Prudish Reporters in Post-Prison Media Frenzy," *Sterogum*, 2013. http://www.stereogum. com/1614372/pussy-riot-face-dumb-questions-prudish-reporters-in-post-prison-media-frenzy/video/

18. Ivan Nezamiatnyi, "Putin pro Pussy Riot: znahit devchonki talntlivye. Prezident prokommentiroval prigovor uchastnitsam gruppy," *Moskovskii komsomolets*, October 8, 2012.

## Chapter 10

1. Max Hayward, *On Trial: The Soviet State versus "Abram Tertz" and "Nikolai Arzhak"* (New York: Harper & Row, 1966).

2. "Russian Conservatives Try to Regulate Halloween, Again." *The Moscow Times,* October 30, 2018. https://www.themoscowtimes.com/2018/10/30/russian-conservatives-try-regulate-halloween-again-a63347

3. Sobchak and Sokolova (2012); Tolokonnikova (2018); Il'ia Zhigulev, "Nadia shila flag na Bolotnoi. A ia sidela v Luganske." Interv'iu Marii Alexinoi o novyx klipakh Pussy Riot, teatre и psikhiatricheskikh bol'nitsah," *Meduza*, November 16, 2016. https://meduza.io/feature/2016/11/06/nadya-shila-flag-na-bolotnoy-a-ya-sidela-v-luganske; Olya Zikrata, "The Affective Work of Sound: The Case of Pussy Riot." *Canadian Slavonic Papers* 60 (3–4) (2018): 571–591.

4. José Alaniz, *Komiks: Comic Art in Russia* (Columbia: University Press of Mississippi, 2014).

5. Some of the characters published by Bubble Comics (founded in 2011) come close to the superhero archetype. In 2017, Sarik Andreasyan attempted a Russian cinematic analogue to The Avengers, called *The Defenders (Zashchitniki)*, but it was a critical and commercial flop.

6. Umberto Eco, "The Myth of Superman," in *Contemporary Literary Criticism: Modernism through Poststructuralism*, ed. Robert Con Davis (New York: Longman, 286), 330–344; Geoff Klock, *How to Read Superhero Comics and Why* (New York: Continuum, 2002).

7. Elena Kostiuchenko, "Kakovo byt' Pussy Riot?" *Novaia gazeta*, August 20, 2012. http://dlib.eastview.com/browse/doc/27550016

8. Mark Lipovetsky, *Postmodern Crises: From "Lolita" to Pussy Riot* (Boston: Academic Studies Press, 2017); Peter Rutland, "The Pussy Riot Affair: Gender and National Identity in Putin's Russia." *The Journal of Nationalism and Ethnicity*, 42.4 (2014): 575–582; Mikhail Iampol'skii, "Tri sloia testa na

odnu izvilinu vlasti," *Novoe vremia*, August 20, 2012. https://newtimes.ru/articles/detail/55977

9. Kevin M.F. Platt, Bela Shayevich, Nadezhda Tolokonnikova, "Pussy Riot Denied Parole," *n+1*. August 1, 2013. https://nplusonemag.com/online-only/online-only/pussy-riot-denied-parole/

10. Kseniia Sobchak, "Tolokonnikova: 'Vystuplenie v khrame bylo oshibkoi.' Alekhina: 'Net, ne beylo.' Interviiu Ksenii Sobchak," *Sobchak zhivem*, December 25, 2013. https://tvrain.ru/teleshow/sobchak_zhivem/tolokonnikova_vystuplenie_v_hrame_bylo_oshibkoj_alehina_net_ne_bylo_intervju_ksenii_sobchak_chast_1-359528/

11. Helena Goscilo and Vlad Strukov, "Introduction," in *Celebrity and Glamour in Contemporary Russia: Shocking Chic*, ed. Helena Goscilo and Vlad Strukov (New York: Routledge, 2011), 1–26.

12. Arkadii Mamontov, "Spetsial'nyi korrespondent. Provokatory 3." https://www.youtube.com/watch?v=dnTjEpSBMdI

13. Claire Bigg and Natalya Dzhanpoladova, "Who Owns the Pussy Riot Brand?" *The Atlantic*, November, 2012. https://www.theatlantic.com/international/archive/2012/11/who-owns-the-pussy-riot-brand/264486/

14. Garadzha Matveeva, "Razgovor Petra Verzilova i Marka Feigina v mae 2012 goda." June 3, 2015.

15. "Priamaia liniia s Tolokonnikovoi i Alekhinoi: o Khodorkovskom, Putine i novom proekte. Polnaia versiia. Chast' 1," (2013). TV Rain, December 27, 2013. https://tvrain.ru/lite/teleshow/experiment/prjamaja_linija_s_tolokonnikovoj_i_alehinoj_o_hodorkovskom_putine_i_novom_proekte_polnaja_versija_chast_1-359653/

16. Pussy Riot. "An Open Letter from Pussy Riot," Common Dreams, February 6, 2015. https://www.commondreams.org/views/2014/02/06/open-letter-pussy-riot

17. Roland Barthes, *Image-Music-Text*, (New York: Hill and Wang, 1978); Michel Foucault, "What Is an Author?" In *Language, Counter-Memory, Practice: Selected Essays and Interviews*, ed. Donald F. Bouchard, trans. Donald F. Bouchard and Sherry Simon (Ithaca: Cornell University Press, 1977), 113–38.

18. Natalya Krainova, "'Pussy Riot' to Be Brand Name," *The Moscow Times*, August 22, 2012; Grigorii Tumanov, Grigorii and Aleksandr Voronov, "Pussy Riot ne dali zotovarit'sia," *Kommersant Daily,* November 3, 2012.

19. Slavoj Zizek, *First as Tragedy, Then as Farce* (New York: Verso, 2009), 51–53.

20. Sperling notes that Pussy Riot "particularly resented the implication that their project had been masterminded by Tolokonnikova's husband,

Petr Verzilov. They explained that it would be 'contradictory to the ideas of feminism if they were fronting for some man'" (2014, 220). Even Pussy Riot's allies fell into the trap of traditional gender roles; as Elena Gapova points out, their defenders in the media repeatedly called for mercy specifically because the prisoners were women (and two of them were mothers of small children); "Delo 'Pusy Riot': feministskij protest v kontekste klassovoj bor'by," *Neprikosnovennyi zapas* 85 (May 2013).

21. Maksim Solius, "Veshch'nedeli: Balaklava Pussy Riot," *Vedomosti*, August 24, 2012.

22. Elena Iakovleva, "Krestovyi pokhod," *Rossiiskaia gazeta*, March 12, 2015.

23. This did not prevent Dugin from asserting that the defendants are an "instrument of the devil" and should be "burned at the stake" ("Kakogo nakazaniia zasluzhivaiut Pussy Riot?" *Komsomol'skaia Pravda*, March 14, 2012.)

## Chapter 11

1. Anastasiia Rodionova, "Porozhdenie Pussi: chto sluchilos' s uchastnikami skandal'nogo pank-molebna. Pussy Riot spustia piat' let posle oglasheniia prigovora," *Moskovskij komsomolets,* August 16, 2017. https://www.mk.ru/social/2017/08/16/porozhdennye-pussi-chto-sluchilos-s-uchastnikami-skandalnogo-pankmolebna.html; Iuliia Taratuta "5 let pank-molebnu: Rasskazyvaiut Tolokonnikova, Alekhina i Samutsevich. Uchastnitsy Pussy Riot o zhizni posle vystupleniia v khrame." *Wonderzine*, February 13, 2017. https://www.wonderzine.com/wonderzine/life/life/224264-pussy-riot

2. "Priamaia liniia (2013)."

3. "Priamaia liniia (2013)."

4. Jonathan Weber, "Pussy Riot Founder Sets Sites on Russian Media." Reuters May 9, 2016. https://www.reuters.com/article/us-russia-pussyriot-media-idUSKCN0Y01M4

5. Luke Harding and Peter Verzilov, "Pussy Riot: Q&A with Nadya Tolokonnikova and Masha Alyokhina," *The Guardian*, February 18, 2015. https://www.theguardian.com/world/2015/feb/18/pussy-riot-i-cant-breathe-nadya-tolokonnikova-masha-alyokhina

6. Luke Harding, "Russian Punk Band Pussy Riot Release I Can't Breathe, Inspired by Eric Garner," *The Guardian*, February 18, 2015. https://www.theguardian.com/world/2015/feb/18/russian-punk-band-pussy-riot-i-cant-breathe-song-eric-garner

## Notes

7. In *Over Her Dead Body*, Elisabeth Bronfen examines 200 years of Western cultural production fascinated with the female corpse, which is usually viewed and/or mourned by the male viewer. One could argue that, in voluntarily placing herself in the position of corpse at the end of an artwork she herself produced, Nadya is playing with this misogynist trope, much like she claims to be "playing with capitalism" when offering up her body for a fashion photoshoot: Elisabeth Bronfen, *Over Her Dead Body: Death, Femininity and the Aesthetic* (New York: Routledge, 1992).

8. Isabella Biedenharn, "'*House of Cards*' Postmortem: Pussy Riot's Masha Alekhina Talks Acting on Her Favorite Show," EW, March 6, 2015. https://ew.com/article/2015/03/06/house-cards-postmortem-pussy-riots-masha-alekhina-tells-how-russian-activists/

9. Olesia Gerasimenko, "Kak teper' zhivet Petr Verzilov—samyi uspeshnyi prodiuser Rossii," April 6, 2017. https://www.gq.ru/heroes/verzilov

10. Lizzie Crocker, "She's in Pussy Riot. He's on the Far Right: How Maria Alyokhina and Dmitry Enteo Fell in Love," *The Daily Beast* (October 16, 2017). https://www.thedailybeast.com/shes-in-pussy-riot-hes-on-the-far-right-how-maria-alyokhina-and-dmitry-enteo-fell-in-love; Olesia Gerasimenko, "Liubit' koshchunnitsu," Batenka.ru. October 11, 2017. https://batenka.ru/resource/sexy/enteo-alekhina/

11. Pussy Riot, "Aktsiia! Aktsiia! Pussi Raiot likvidatsiia! Pussi Raiot iz ded!" May 22, 2015. https://pussy-riot.livejournal.com/34906.html

12. Pussy Riot, "Aktsiia!," (2015).

13. Pussy Riot. "Ia ubila protest!!!!" March 4, 2024. https://pussy-riot.livejournal.com/6786.html

14. Pussy Riot, "Ia ubila."

## Conclusion

1. "Russian experimental theater director arrested on Red Square for holding poster that reads 'Against the Stanislavsky method,'" *Meduza*, May 31, 2019. https://meduza.io/en/news/2019/05/31/russian-experimental-theater-director-arrested-on-red-square-for-holding-poster-that-reads-against-the-stanislavsky-method.

2. Marc Bennets, "Hundreds arrested in Moscow During Protest over Ivan Golunov," *The Guardian*, June 15, 2019. https://www.theguardian.com/world/2019/jun/12/hundreds-arrested-in-moscow-protests-over-arrest-ivan-golunov-investigative-journalist; Zhigulev (2016).

3. Mikhail Ryklin, "Pussy Riot voshli v istoriiu bor'by s rezhimom Putina," DW.com, March 21, 2016. https://www.dw.com/ru/михаил-рыклин-pussy-riot-вошли-в-историю-борьбы-с-режимом-путина/a-19130538

4. Anastasiia Rodionova, "Porozhdenie Pussi: chto sluchilos' s uchastnikami skandal'nogo pank-molebna. Pussy Riot spustia piat' let posle oglasheniia prigovora," *Moskovskij komsomolets*, August 16, 2017. https://www.mk.ru/social/2017/08/16/porozhdennye-pussi-chto-sluchilos-s-uchastnikami-skandalnogo-pankmolebna.html; Taratuta (2017).

5. Masha Gessen, *Words Will Break Cement: The Passion of Pussy Riot* (New York: Riverhead Books, 2014), 88–90.

6. Katerina Clark, *The Soviet Novel: History as Ritual*, 3rd edn (Bloomington: Indiana University Press, 2000).

# SELECTED BIBLIOGRAPHY

## Articles and books

Alyohina, Maria, *Riot Days*. (New York: Metropolitan Books, 2017).

Bernstein, Anya, "An Inadvertent Sacrifice: Body Politics and Sovereign Power in the Pussy Riot Affair," *Critical Inquiry* 40 (1): 220–241. https://criticalinquiry.uchicago.edu/an_inadvertent_sacrifice_body_politics_and_sovereign_power_in_the_pussy_rio/

Beumers, Birgit, Alexander Etkind, Olga Gurov, and Sanna Turoma (eds.), *Cultural Forms of Protest in Russia* (New York: Routledge, 2017).

Bruce, Caitlin, "The Balaclava as Affect Generator: Free Pussy Riot Protests and Transnational Iconicity," *Communications and Critical/Cultural Studies* 12.1 (2015): 42–52.

Chehonadskih, Maria, "What is Pussy Riot's 'Idea'?" *Radical Philosophy* 176 (Nov/Dec 2012). https://www.radicalphilosophy.com/commentary/what-is-pussy-riots-idea

Denysenko, Nicholas, "An Appeal to Mary: An Analysis of Pussy Riot's Punk Performance in Moscow," *Journal of the American Academy of Religion* 81.4 (2013): 1061–1092.

Dzero, Irina and Bystrova, Tatyana, "Pussy Riot and the Translatability of Cultures," *Transcultural Studies* 13.2 (2017): 264–286.

Gabowitsch, Mischa, *Protest in Putin's Russia*. (New York: Polity, 2017).

Galeotti, Mark, *We Need to Talk About Putin: Why the West Gets Him Wrong, and How to Get Him Right* (New York: Ebury Press, 2019).

Gapova, Elena, "Becoming Visible in the Digital Age: The Class and Media Dimensions of the Pussy Riot Affair," *Feminist Media Studies* 15.1 (2015).

Gessen, Masha, *Words Will Break Cement: The Passion of Pussy Riot* (New York: Riverhead Books, 2014).

Jonson, Lena, "Post-Pussy Riot: Art and Protest in Russia Today," *Nationalities Papers* 44.5 (2016): 657–672.

Korte, Anne-Marie, Zorgdrager, Heleen and Tolstaya, Katya (eds.), *Special Issue on Pussy Riot's Punk Prayer, Religion and Gender* 4.2 (2014).

Kotkin, Stephen, *Armageddon Averted: The Soviet Collapse, 1970–2000* (Oxford: Oxford University Press, 2008).

Lipovetsky, Mark, "Pussy Riot as the Trickstar," *Postmodern Crises: From "Lolita" to Pussy Riot* (Boston: Academic Studies Press, 2017).

## Selected Bibliography

Mendelevich, Vladimir D., "The Extraordinary Case of Russian Performance Artist Pyotr Pavlensky: Psychopathology or Contemporary Art?" *Transcultural Psychiatry* 56.3 (June 2018): 569–585.

Moss, Kevin, "Russia as the Saviour of European Civilization: Gender and The Geopolitics of Traditional Values," in *Anti-Gender Campaigns in Europe: Mobilizing against Equality*, ed. Roman Kuhar and David Paternotte (London: Rowan & Littlefield, 2017), 195–214.

Nelson, Ingrid, "Artist for a New Age: Dissident Russian Performance Art and the Work of Petr Pavlenskii," *Russian Literature* 96–98 (2018): 277–295.

Prozorov, Sergei, "Pussy Riot and the Politics of Profanation: Parody, Performativity, Veridiction," *Political Studies* 62.4 (2014): 766–783.

Rourke, Brian and Wiget, Andrew, "Pussy Riot, Putin and the Politics of Embodiment," *Cultural Studies* 30.2 (2016): 234–260.

Rutland, Peter (ed.), *Special Section: Pussy Riot. Nationalities Papers* 42.4 (2014): 575–636.

Seal, Lizzie, "Pussy Riot and Feminist Cultural Criminology: A New 'Femininity in Dissent'?" *Contemporary Justice Review* 16.2 (2013): 293–303.

Sperling, Valerie, *Sex, Politics, and Putin: Political Legitimacy in Russia* (Oxford: Oxford University Press, 2014)

Steinholt, Yngvar B., "Kitten Heresy: Lost Contexts of Pussy Riot's Punk Prayer," *Popular Music and Society* 36.1 (2013): 120–124.

Suchland, Jennifer, "Contextualizing Pussy Riot in Russia and Beyond," *E-International Relations*, August 28, 2012. https://www.e-ir. info/2012/08/28/contextualizing-pussy-riot-in-russia-and-beyond/.

Tolokonnikova, Nadya, *Read and Riot: A Pussy Riot Guide to Activism* (New York: HarperOne, 2018).

Tuttle, Tara, "Deranged Vaginas: Pussy Riot's Feminist Hermeneutics," *Journal of Religion and Popular Culture* 28.2–3 (2016): 67–80.

Willems, Joachim, "Why 'Punk'? Religion, Anarchism and Feminism in Pussy Riot's *Punk Prayer*," Religion, State and Society 42.4 (2014): 403–419.

Zabyelina, Yuliya and Ivashkiv, Roman, "Pussy Riot and the Politics of Resistance in Contemporary Russia," *The Oxford Encyclopedia of Crime, Media and Popular Culture*, ed. Nicole Rafter and Michelle Brown (Oxford: Oxford University Press, 2018).

Zikrata, Olya, "The Affective Work of Sound: The Case of Pussy Riot's Noise," Canadian Slavonic Papers 60.3–4 (2018): 571–591.

## Film

*Pussy Riot: A Punk Prayer*, dir. Mike Lerner and Maxim Pozdorovkin, 2013.

# INDEX

# Index

# Index